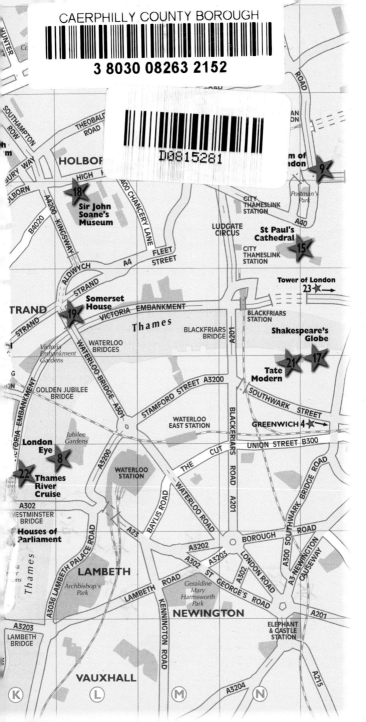

HOLBORN

Sir John Soane's Museum **18**

LUDGATE CIRCUS

St Paul's Cathedral **15**

9

CITY THAMESLINK STATION

CITY THAMESLINK STATION

Postman's Park

Tower of London **23** →

STRAND

19 Somerset House

VICTORIA EMBANKMENT

Thames

WATERLOO BRIDGES

BLACKFRIARS BRIDGE

BLACKFRIARS STATION

Shakespeare's Globe

Victoria Embankment Gardens

GOLDEN JUBILEE BRIDGE

21 **17** Tate Modern

SOUTHWARK STREET

GREENWICH 4 →

Jubilee Gardens

STAMFORD STREET A3200

WATERLOO EAST STATION

UNION STREET B300

London Eye **8**

22 Thames River Cruise

WATERLOO STATION

THE CUT

WESTMINSTER BRIDGE

Houses of Parliament

LAMBETH

Archbishop's Park

Geraldine Mary Harmsworth Park

NEWINGTON

ELEPHANT & CASTLE STATION

LAMBETH BRIDGE

VAUXHALL

CITYPACK GUIDE TO
London

Contents

KEY TO SYMBOLS

- Map reference to the accompanying pull-out map
- ✉ Address
- ☎ Telephone number
- 🕐 Opening/closing times
- 🍴 Restaurant or café
- 🚉 Nearest rail station
- Ⓜ Nearest Tube (subway) station
- 🚌 Nearest bus route

ENTERTAINMENT 128

Whether you're after a cultural fix or just want a place to relax with a drink after a hard day's sight-seeing, we've made the best choices for you.

EAT 140

Uncover great dining experiences, from a quick bite at lunch to top-notch evening meals.

SLEEP 152

We've brought together the best hotels in the city, whatever budget you're on.

NEED TO KNOW 160

The practical information you need to make your trip run smoothly.

PULL-OUT MAP

The fold-out map accompanying this book is a comprehensive street plan of the city. We've given grid references within the book for each sight and listing.

🛳 Nearest riverboat or ferry stop

♿ Facilities for visitors with disabilities

ℹ Tourist information

❓ Other practical information

💷 Admission charges: Expensive (over £10), Moderate (£5–£10) and Inexpensive (under £5)

▷ Further information

Introducing London

Prepare for London to challenge your expectations. The dynamic British capital's traditions, from Savile Row outfitters to parading Horse Guards, thrive alongside a cutting-edge cultural calendar, arts venues, museums and world-class restaurants.

London buzzes with energy as whole areas of the capital have been revitalized. Spectacular modern architecture soars above ancient buildings. The cleaning of St. Paul's Cathedral has revealed its true glory; Tate Modern provides great spaces in which to enjoy contemporary art; and the Millennium Footbridge, spanning the Thames between the two sights, gives a modern edge to one of the world's best panoramic city views. Along the river, trendy restaurants fill renovated warehouses, and gardens, museums, markets, theatre and arts complexes have regenerated the South Bank.

In the redeveloped Docklands, the old Port of London is now a glittering world of skyscrapers, dominated by the innovative Canary Wharf, while construction of the Docklands Light Railway (DLR) has revolutionized the transport system. Building for the 2012 Olympic Games has transformed districts further east.

Amid all this change, the greatness of London's 2,000 years of history has not been quashed. Visitors can still roam around one of Britain's finest medieval forts, the Tower of London, or visit a real royal home, Buckingham Palace. Equally, you can picnic in one of the royal parks or take a boat ride along the Thames to evoke times when this was the backbone of London and its great port.

Londoners themselves—while appreciating their good-value theatre, free museums, great buildings and wealth of traditions—are likely to moan about just about everything else, from the high cost of property and living to the Congestion Charge and over-crowded public transport. Yet, in truth, they know they are living in the world's greatest and most vibrant city. London, the political, financial and artistic capital of Britain, is hard to beat. Everything you could ever want is here; it is up to you to take it and enjoy it.

FACTS AND FIGURES

- Greater London covers 1,584sq km (611sq miles). With a population of over 8.17 million, it is Europe's largest city.
- London is the most culturally diverse city in Britain and more than 300 languages are spoken in the capital.
- London is the only city to have hosted the Summer Olympics three times (1908, 1948 and 2012).

CITY WITHIN A CITY

The City of London covers about 2.5sq km (1sq mile) and is Europe's largest central business and financial district. Referred to by Londoners either as 'The City' or 'The Square Mile', it has a daily working population that swells to over 300,000. The City has its own administration and police force and every year elects its own Lord Mayor.

DOWN UNDER

The London Underground ('the Tube') is the oldest underground rail network in the world. The first line opened in 1863: 6km (4 miles) between Paddington and Farringdon Street on the Metropolitan Line. Today the London Underground carries more than 1 billion passengers per year on 11 lines covering 402km (249 miles) of track and serving 270 stations.

BEATING THE COSTS

London is expensive. So, start by working out what is free. Top of the list are most major museums and galleries, the parks, monuments such as churches, and a variety of entertainment including lunchtime concerts and other events. To cut unavoidable costs, buy a Travel Pass and perhaps the London Sightseeing Pass (www.londonpass.com).

Focus On the Olympic Legacy

The regeneration of east London, with the creation of new housing, parks and sports facilities, is the lasting legacy of London's role as host city of the 2012 Olympic and Paralympic Games.

The Gift of Regeneration

While central London received a major facelift for the Millennium and the glittering, high-rise financial hub that is Docklands has risen, phoenix-like, from the previously derelict and desolate docks, hosting the 2012 Olympics brought the opportunity to transform a socially deprived and economically depressed area in the east of the city.

London's successful bid focused heavily on urban regeneration and the promise to make the Olympic Park a blueprint for sustainable living. As a result, one of the largest urban parks in Europe was created. Planted with native tree species and including a new wetland habitat formed from the canals and waterways of the River Lea, it links the tidal Thames Estuary and the surrounding Hertfordshire countryside.

Building on Tradition

Inspiration for this '21st-century garden city' came from London's existing city-centre parks and garden squares—think Hyde Park (▷ 71) and St. James's Park (▷ 40)—with modern versions of traditional Georgian and Victorian squares, crescents and terraces within walking distance of open spaces. Riverside properties are springing up along the banks of rejuvenated waterways. Schools, nurseries and shops, as well as faith, health and community centres, are all part of the family-focused mix.

Olympic Legacy

The Athletes' Village, northeast of the Stadium, is being converted into homes. East Village, with its shops, bars, cafés and restaurants,

Clockwise from top: A section of the Lea Valley Walk; a sign for the Greenway, a traffic-free path by London's Olympic Park; an artist's impression of ArcelorMittal

opened in 2013 and a further five distinctive new neighbourhoods with up to 8,000 homes are planned over the next 20 years.

Queen Elizabeth Olympic Park

Londoners are now enjoying the former Olympic site and its facilities, which was renamed the Queen Elizabeth Olympic Park in 2013 to celebrate the Queen's Diamond Jubilee. Attractions include the entertainment plaza planned for the south of the park, around the Stadium; the Stadium itself, which is destined to become the new home of West Ham United football club; and the impressive Aquatics Centre, with two 50m (55yd) swimming pools. In the north of the park, waterways, expansive parkland and green space feature and Londoners are able to explore play areas, walking routes and cycle paths in the Lea River Valley. The Olympic Velodrome will become the hub of a new Velopark, an area including 6km (3.7 miles) of mountain-bike trails, a road-cycle circuit and off-road trails.

ArcelorMittal Orbit

ArcelorMittal Orbit, an observational tower 114m (374ft) high, designed by artist Anish Kapoor, is another lasting monument to the Games. Visitors to the Olympic Park are able to climb the sculpture, a looping lattice of tubular steel, to enjoy views of the park and the London skyline from its viewing platforms.

Improved Infrastructure

The area has benefited from the new transport links created by the Docklands Light Railway (DLR), the extended East London Line, improvements to the Underground system and better access at both Stratford International and Stratford Regional train stations, where nine rail lines link the area to central London, Britain and Europe.

Orbit; the Docklands Light Railway (DLR); a sign for the CS3 route of the Cycle Superhighway; Stratford Station, main access point to the Olympic Park

Top Tips For...

These great suggestions will help you tailor your ideal visit to London, no matter how you choose to spend your time.

...Serious Retail Therapy

Start on the ground floor of **Harrods** (▷ 125) and work up, collecting Harrods shopping bags as you go.

Be girlie: spend a whole day in **Harvey Nichols** (▷ 125) or **Selfridges** (▷ 126).

Search **Liberty** (▷ 126) for a range of indulgent accessories.

Make a weekend foray into the five markets of the **Camden Markets** (▷ 124).

Tempt your tastebuds at **Borough Market's** (▷ 67) wonderful array of organic and artisan food stalls.

...A Meal With a View

Book a table at the **Portrait Restaurant** atop the National Portrait Gallery (▷ 150).

Rendezvous at the café on level 6 of **Tate Modern** (▷ 151).

Go to Canary Wharf to eat at the waterside **The Gun** (▷ 147).

Splash out at **Rhodes Twenty Four** (▷ 150), with a cocktail 18 floors above at **Vertigo 42**.

Eat stylishly amid trees and flamingos at rooftop **Babylon** (▷ 144).

...A Breath of Fresh Air

Roam **Hampstead Heath** (▷ 77) and visit **Kenwood House** (▷ 77).

Climb high in **Greenwich Park** (▷ 20–21) to enjoy London views.

Enjoy botanical riches from around the world at **Kew Gardens** (▷ 77).

Go boating in **Regent's Park** (▷ 72) and visit the zoo.

Do the great central London royal park walk: through **St. James's** (▷ 40–41), **Green** (▷ 70) and **Hyde Park** (▷ 71), then **Kensington Gardens** (▷ 24–25).

Clockwise from top: Harrods—the ultimate department store; the Great Court of the British Museum; crowds gather to watch the Changing the Guard ceremony at

...After Dark

Jazz Café, **Jazz After Dark** (▷ 135) and **Pizza Express Club Soho** (▷ 137) for quality jazz.
Check out **Scala** (▷ 138) in the redeveloped area around King's Cross.
Dance the night away at **Guanabara** (▷ 135).
Barfly (▷ 133) in Camden showcases the indie scene with several acts nightly.
Head south of the river to the **Ministry of Sound** (▷ 136) for high-energy clubbing.

...Watching the Bank Balance

Stay at funky and inexpensive **Clink 261** (▷ 156) backpackers' hostel.
Head to **Gaby's Deli** (▷ 146) on Charing Cross Road for hearty, no-nonsense food.
Go to a free concert in a church such as **St. Margaret**, **Lothbury** (▷ 74).
Buy your theatre tickets at **'tkts'** in Leicester Square (▷ 136).
Visit a free museum such as the **British Museum** (▷ 16–17).

...Peeking Inside Londoners' Homes

Dr. Johnson's house (▷ 69), where he compiled his dictionary.
Sir John Soane's two houses (▷ 48–49), filled with his antiquities.
Handel House (▷ 70), the German composer's home for 26 years.
Buckingham Palace (▷ 18–19), the Queen's London home.
Spencer House (▷ 74), the aristocratic Spencer family's mansion.

...Keeping the Kids Happy

Handle objects at the hands-on tables in the **British Museum** (▷ 16–17).
Climb the steps to the top of **St. Paul's Cathedral** (▷ 42).
Go boating in **Regent's Park** (▷ 72).
Explore the hands-on exhibits at the Launch Pad in the **Science Museum** (▷ 45).

Buckingham Palace; the Making the Modern World gallery at the Science Musuem; time out in Green Park; the 19th-century Palm House at Kew Gardens

Timeline

1042 Edward the Confessor becomes king, making London the capital of England and Westminster his home; builds the abbey church of St. Peter.

1066 The Norman king, William the Conqueror, defeats King Harold at the Battle of Hastings; begins the Tower of London.

1485 Tudor rule commences, ending in 1603 with the death of Elizabeth I.

1533 Henry VIII breaks with Rome to marry Anne Boleyn; establishes the Church of England.

1649 Charles I is executed in Whitehall; the Commonwealth (1649–53) and Protectorate (1653–59) govern England until Charles II is restored to the throne in 1660.

1666 The Great Fire of London.

1759 The British Museum, London's first public museum, opens.

1851 The Great Exhibition is held in Hyde Park.

1863 World's first urban underground train service opens. In 1890 the first deep-dug train runs (known as 'the Tube').

1939–45 Blitz bombings destroy a

EARLY LONDON

● Emperor Claudius invades Britain in AD43; a deep-water port, Londinium, is soon established.

● In the year 200 the Romans put a wall around Londinium, now capital of Britannia Superior; they withdraw in 410.

THE GREAT FIRE

The fire broke out at a baker's near Pudding Lane on the night of 2 September 1666. Raging for four days and nights, it destroyed four-fifths of the City of London and 13,200 homes. Sir Christopher Wren became the grand architect of the subsequent rebuilding of the city.

The London's Burning exhibit in the Museum of London shows the devastation caused by the fire

An attack by Luftwaffe bombers during the Blitz

third of the City of London and much of the docks.

1951 Festival of Britain held on the site of the South Bank arts complex.

1960s The Beatles, Carnaby Street and the King's Road help create 'swinging London'.

1981 Regeneration and development of London Docklands begins.

1994 First Eurostar trains link London and Paris through the Channel Tunnel.

2000 Ken Livingstone is elected as the first mayor of all London. Major millennium projects rejuvenate central London.

2002 Queen Elizabeth II celebrates her Golden Jubilee.

2003 Clarence House, formerly the Queen Mother's home, first opens to the public during the summer months.

2007 Eurostar trains use refurbished St. Pancras station, no longer Waterloo.

2011 Prince William and Catherine Middleton are married at Westminster Abbey.

2012 London celebrates: the city hosts the Olympic Games and marks the Queen's Diamond Jubilee.

2013 Birth of HRH Prince George, third in line to the throne.

GROWING CITY

● During the 16th century, London was Europe's fastest-growing city; its population rose from 75,000 to 200,000.
● By 1750, London was Europe's biggest and wealthiest city, with about 700,000 people.
● London's population continued to grow, from around 1 million in 1800 to 6.5 million by 1900, peaking during World War II at 9 million.
● The city's population is currently over 8 million and rising.

The Great Exhibition of 1851

The new Eurostar terminal at St. Pancras station

★ Top 25

This section contains the must-see Top 25 sights and experiences in London. They are listed alphabetically, and numbered so you can locate them on the inside front cover map.

1 Banqueting House

HIGHLIGHTS

- Rubens ceiling
- Allegory of James I between Peace and Plenty
- Allegory of the birth and coronation of Charles I
- Weathercock put on the roof by James II
- Vaulted undercroft, a drinking den for James I
- Whitehall river terrace in Embankment Gardens
- Video and self-guided audio tour

It is chilling to imagine Charles I calmly crossing the park from St. James's Palace to be beheaded outside the glorious hall built by his father. The magnificent ceiling was painted for Charles by Flemish artist Peter Paul Rubens.

Magnificent rooms This, all that remains of Whitehall Palace, was London's first building to be coated in smooth white Portland stone. Designed by Inigo Jones and built between 1619 and 1622, it marked the beginning of James I's dream to replace the original sprawling Tudor palace with a 2,000-room Palladian masterpiece. In fact, it was only the banqueting hall that was built. Inside, the King hosted small parties in the crypt and presided over lavish court ceremonies upstairs.

Clockwise from far left: The main hall, with ceiling paintings by Rubens; the elegant neoclassical exterior; a bust of Charles I, who was executed outside the Banqueting House in 1649; Rubens's nine allegorical ceiling paintings, which depict the unification of Scotland and England

Rubens ceiling The stunning ceiling was commissioned by James's son, Charles I. Painted between 1634 and 1636 by Peter Paul Rubens, the panels celebrate James I, who was also James VI of Scotland. Nine allegorical paintings show the unification of Scotland and England and the joyous benefits of wise rule. Rubens waited two years for his £3,000 fee.

The demise The palace has had a fair share of bad luck. Cardinal Thomas Wolsey lived so ostentatiously that he fell from Henry VIII's grace. Henry made it his, and his successors', main London royal home. Charles I was beheaded here on 30 January 1649, and William III suffered from the dank river air. A fire in 1698 wiped out the Tudor building, leaving only the Banqueting House.

THE BASICS

www.hrp.org.uk

🔹 K6

✉ Whitehall, SW1

☎ 0844 482 7777

🕐 Mon–Sun 10–5; last admission 4.15. Closed 24 Dec–1 Jan, public hols and for functions and events

🚇 Westminster, Charing Cross, Embankment

♿ None

💷 Moderate

❓ Occasional lunchtime and evening concerts

HIGHLIGHTS

● Enlightenment Gallery
● Oriental antiquities
● African Galleries
● Rosetta Stone
● Living and Dying Gallery
● Elgin Marbles
● Assyrian and Egyptian rooms
● The King's Library
● Norman Foster's Great Court redevelopment

TIPS

● Pick up a plan in the Great Court and choose just a few rooms to explore.
● Take an Eye Opener tour.
● Do the Hands-On object handling.
● Rent an audio guide.

The collection here is truly breathtaking, with a wealth of ancient treasures, among them bronzes from the Indian Chola dynasty and the lion-filled reliefs that once lined the walls of an Assyrian palace.

Physician founder Sir Hans Sloane, after whom Sloane Square is named, was a fashionable London physician, 'interested in the whole of human knowledge' and an avid collector of everything from plants to prints. When he died in 1753 aged 92 he left his collection of more than 71,000 objects to the nation on condition that it was given a permanent home. Thus began the British Museum, opened in 1759 in a 17th-century mansion, Britain's first public museum and now its largest, covering 5.5ha (13.5 acres), with eight million objects.

Clockwise from far left: The Queen Elizabeth II Great Court, designed by Foster and Partners as part of a redevelopment in the late 1990s; the historic circular Reading Room, at the heart of the Great Court; exhibits in the museum's Egyptian collection; the museum's imposing main entrance

Expansion George II, George III and George IV added to Sloane's collection, as did other monarchs. Their gifts, combined with the Townley and Elgin Marbles, burst the building's seams, and so architect Robert Smirke designed a new museum, completed by his son, Sydney, in 1857. Even so, with booty from expeditions and excavations pouring in, the natural history collections moved to South Kensington (▷ 36–37). When the British Library (▷ 67) moved to St. Pancras in 1998, the Great Court was redeveloped and the King's Library transformed into a gallery on the Enlightenment.

Starting to explore Head to the glass-and-steel-roofed Great Court, a magnificent space with an education centre, lecture theatres, seminar rooms and cafés, to get your bearings.

THE BASICS

www.britishmuseum.org

🔲 J3

✉ Great Russell Street, WC1 (another entrance in Montague Place)

☎ 020 7323 8299

🕐 Galleries: Sun–Thu 10–5.30, Fri 10–8.30. Great Court: Sun–Thu 9–6, Fri 9–8.30. Closed 24–26 Dec, 1 Jan

🍴 Restaurant, cafés

🚇 Holborn, Tottenham Court Road

♿ Very good

🎟 Free, except for some temporary exhibitions

❓ Full educational schedule

3 Buckingham Palace

HIGHLIGHTS

- The Queen's Gallery
- Changing the Guard
- State Coach, Royal Mews
- Nash's facade, Quadrangle
- Gobelin tapestries in the Guard Room
- Throne Room
- Van Dyck's portrait of Charles I and family

TIPS

- To avoid the lines, book a timed ticket in advance.
- Visit the quality royal souvenir shops.

Of the capital's houses now open to visitors, the Queen's London home is perhaps the most fascinating: Where else can you see a living sovereign's private art collection, drawing rooms and horse harnesses?

Yet another palace British sovereigns have had homes all over London over the years; moving from Westminster to Whitehall to Kensington and St. James's, and finally to Buckingham Palace. It was George III who bought the prime-site mansion, Buckingham House, in 1761 as a gift for his new bride, the 17-year-old Queen Charlotte, leaving St. James's Palace to be the official royal residence.

Grand improvements King George IV and his architect John Nash made extravagant changes

Clockwise from far left: Buckingham Palace is the London home of the British sovereign—the red, gold and blue Royal Standard is raised when the Queen is in residence; visitors at the palace gates; the Grand Staircase, designed by John Nash; the Mall, the ceremonial route to the palace

using Bath stone, later covered up by Edward Blore's facade added for Queen Victoria. Today, the 600 rooms and 16ha (40-acre) garden include the State Apartments, offices for the Royal Household, a cinema, swimming pool and the Queen's private rooms.

Open house The Queen inherited the world's finest private art collection. The Queen's Gallery, opened for her Golden Jubilee in 2002, exhibits some of her treasures. In the Royal Mews, John Nash's stables house gleaming fairy-tale coaches, harnesses and other apparel used for royal ceremonies. Don't miss the Buckingham Palace Summer Opening, when visitors can wander through the grand State Rooms resplendent with gold, pictures, porcelain, tapestries and thrones and enjoy the gardens.

THE BASICS

www.royal.gov.uk

➕ G7

✉ Buckingham Gate, SW1

☎ 020 7766 7300; Queen's Gallery 020 7766 7301; Royal Mews 020 7766 7302

◉ Queen's Gallery: daily 9.30–5.30, last admission 4.30. Royal Mews: 2 Jan–29 Mar Mon–Sat 10–4; 30 Mar–31 Oct daily 10–5, 1–30 Nov Mon–Sat 10–4; last admission 45 min before closing. Closed Dec and ceremonial occasions. State Rooms, Buckingham Palace: Aug daily 9.30–7, Sep daily 9.30–6 (last admission 2 hours 15 min before closing)

🚇 Victoria, Hyde Park Corner, Green Park

🚆 Victoria

♿ Excellent

💰 Expensive

❓ No photography

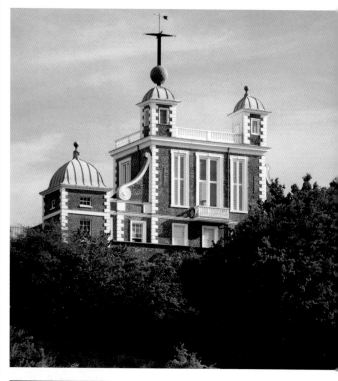

HIGHLIGHTS

● *Captain Augustus Keppel* by Sir Joshua Renolds (Queen's House)
● Maritime equipment at the National Maritime Museum
● Winter star gazing at the Royal Observatory

A UNESCO World Heritage Site, this historic London district is a highly recommended day out, enthralling children and adults with science, sea stories and an excellent art collection. The town itself has a market, restaurants and a park.

Old Royal Naval College and the *Cutty Sark*
Stop first at the *Cutty Sark*, once one of the fastest tea clippers in the world. Ravaged by fire in 2007, it took five years to restore. Continue into the main quadrangle of the Old Royal Naval College. With your back to the Thames, the remarkable Painted Hall, notable for its spectacular ceiling, is on the right.

Art and maritime heritage At the foot of Greenwich Park, the Queen's House and

Clockwise from far left: The Royal Observatory, designed by Sir Christopher Wren; the Greenwich Meridian, the point chosen as 0° longitude; the Cutty Sark's figurehead; the Cutty Sark; the Galvanic Magnetic Clock on the Greenwich Meridian, from which time around the world is measured

National Maritime Museum stand adjacent to each other. The Queen's House is beautifully proportioned but the real surprise is the outstanding art collection inside. The National Maritime Museum is crammed with hands-on exhibits that answer pressing questions such as why the sea is salty. Boats on display range from small dinghies to the *Miss Britain III*, the first powerboat to top 100mph. Don't miss the fascinating collection of navigational equipment.

Astronomical delights Inside Sir Christopher Wren's cramped Observatory, small galleries explain how time is measured. But the new astronomy galleries of the Planetarium next door merit much more time; they're modern, engaging and exciting but don't simplify the bigger questions about the universe.

HIGHLIGHTS

● View from Westminster Bridge
● Big Ben
● Summer tours
● St. Stephen's Hall
● Westminster Hall
● State Opening of Parliament
● Central Lobby

Britain is governed from this landmark building alongside the River Thames. For many visitors, its clock tower and Big Ben chiming the hour symbolize London. Interesting tours reveal its architecture, traditions and the workings of government.

Powerhouse for crown and state William the Conqueror made Westminster his seat of rule to watch over the London merchants. It was soon the heart of government for England, then for Britain, then for a globe-encircling empire. It was also the principal home of the monarchs until Henry VIII moved to Whitehall. Here the foundations of Parliament were laid according to Edward I's Model Parliament of 1295: a combination of elected citizens, lords and clergy. This developed into the House of

Clockwise from top left: A night-time view of the Houses of Parliament from the South Bank; Thomas Thornycroft's early 20th-century bronze of Boadicea by Westminster Bridge; Big Ben and the London Eye; Central Lobby, a meeting place between the House of Commons and the House of Lords

Commons (elected Members of Parliament) and the House of Lords (unelected senior members of State and Church). Henry VIII's Reformation Parliament of 1529–36 ended Church domination of Parliament and made the Commons more powerful than the Lords.

Fit for an empire Having survived the Catholic conspiracy to blow up Parliament on 5 November 1605, most of the buildings were destroyed by a fire in 1834. Kingdom and empire needed a new headquarters. With Charles Barry's plans and A.W. Pugin's detailed design, a masterpiece of Victorian Gothic was created. Behind the facade, the Lords is on the left and the Commons on the right. If Parliament is in session, there is a flag on Victoria Tower or, at night, a light on Big Ben.

THE BASICS

www.parliament.uk

✚ K8

✉ Westminster, SW1

☎ 020 7219 3000;
Commons 020 7219 4272;
Lords 020 7219 3107;
tours 0844 847 1672

🕐 Visits to House of Commons public gallery when house is sitting: Mon 2.30–10.30, Tue 11.30–7.30, Wed 11.30–7.30, Thu 9.30–5.30, Fri 9.30–3. Tours during summer recesses (usually Aug–Sep) and Sat throughout the year 9.15–4.30. Tours take 75 min and depart every 15 min. UK citizens can arrange tours at other times through their MP

🚇 Westminster

🚂 Waterloo

♿ Parliament free; tours expensive

❓ State Opening of Parliament in May

HIGHLIGHTS

- King's Grand Staircase
- Presence Chamber
- Wind dial, King's Gallery
- Luminous Lace light piece
- Princess Victoria's dolls' house
- Royal dresses
- Tea in the Orangery
- Italian Gardens

One of the reasons that King William III moved out of Whitehall Palace and into a mansion in this tiny Kensington village was that he suffered from asthma and was looking for an area with cleaner air.

Perfect location The year he became king, 1689, William and his wife Mary bought their mansion, perfectly positioned for London socializing and country living. They brought in Sir Christopher Wren and Nicholas Hawksmoor to remodel and enlarge the house, and moved in for Christmas.

A special royal home Despite the small rooms, George I introduced palatial grandeur with Colen Campbell's staircase and state rooms. Queen Anne added the Orangery (the

Clockwise from far left: A view of the palace from Dial Walk in Kensington Gardens; a statue commemorating William III, the palace's first royal resident; George Frampton's famed statue of Peter Pan in Kensington Gardens; the Orangery; the peaceful Italian Garden, a Victorian addition

THE BASICS

www.hrp.org.uk

✚ A6

✉ Kensington Gardens, W8

☎ 0844 482 7777; Serpentine Gallery 020 7402 6075; www.serpentinegallery.org

🕐 Daily 10–6; last entry 1 hour before closing. Serpentine Gallery daily 10–6

🍽 Café, Orangery (▷ 149)

🚇 High Street Kensington, Queensway

♿ Good

💷 Expensive; family tickets. Serpentine Gallery free

❓ Personalized tours by expert Explainers

architect was Nicholas Hawksmoor, the wood-carver Grinling Gibbons) and annexed a chunk of royal Hyde Park, a trick repeated by George II's wife, Queen Caroline, who created the Round Pond and Long Water to complete the 110ha (275-acre) Kensington Gardens. Today, a variety of trees are the backdrop for sculptures (George Frampton's fairytale *Peter Pan*, ▷ 72), monuments, and contemporary exhibitions at the Serpentine Gallery.

New look A £12-million project has opened up previously unseen areas of the palace, including fine state apartments and landscaped public gardens. The routes focus on different historical eras and figures, including Diana, Princess of Wales, and Queen Victoria, whose story is told in her own words.

HIGHLIGHTS

● Food halls at Harrods
● Designer dresses at Harvey Nichols
● Boutiques on Walton Street

TIPS

● In Harrods, check out the day's events, shows and demos.
● If you need a special outfit, no staff are more helpful than at Harvey Nichols.
● If it rains, stay put in Harrods and visit the spa.

Knightsbridge is London's smartest and most expensive neighbourhood, with real estate, shops and price tags to match. It's the place for some serious retail therapy.

Stylish shops As you leave the Underground station (Sloane Street exit) you'll see Harvey Nichols (▷ 125), London's most fashionable department store. On emerging from Harvey Nichols, head back towards the Underground and continue along Brompton Road. Opposite is a huge Burberry store, known for its tan-and-grey check designs. On the left, as you walk towards the canopied shopfront of Harrods (▷ 125), is Swarovski, with its window displays of crystal jewellery. Leave Harrods by the Hans Road exit and you'll see lingerie store Rigby & Peller across the street.

Clockwise from far left: Harvey Nichols's flagship Knightsbridge store; Swarovski jewellery shop on Brompton Road; the landmark art nouveau Michelin building, now home to the popular Bibendum restaurant; Harrods; the Fifth Floor Bar at Harvey Nichols

Even more stylish shops Return to Brompton Road and pass leather store Mulberry, before turning left into Beauchamp Place for smart restaurants, designer fashion and the Map House, with its precious maps and engravings. At the end of Beauchamp Place, turn right into attractive Walton Street, lined with interior design, jewellery and children's clothes shops. Ahead you'll see Joseph, which sells stylish women's clothing. With Chanel to your right across Brompton Road, turn left into Sloane Avenue by the iconic Michelin building. The Conran Shop, selling contemporary design for the home, is on the right, with fashion from Paul Smith and Joseph for Men on the left. Continue down Sloane Avenue to reach the King's Road or turn left for Sloane Square, home to Peter Jones, the department store.

THE BASICS

🔹 D7–8
✉ Knightsbridge
🍽 Harvey Nichols' 5th floor is dedicated to food. Go to Harrods for elegant dining and macaroons. The Berkeley Hotel (Wilton Place, tel 020 7235 6000, serves afternoon tea daily 1–5)
🚇 Knightsbridge

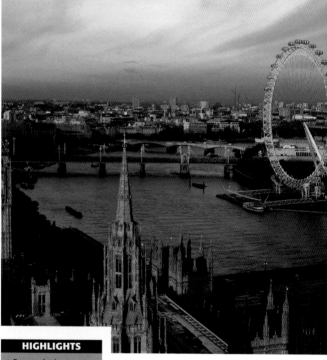

HIGHLIGHTS

● Panoramic views across the city in every direction
● On a clear day you can see for 40km (25 miles)
● Spotting landmarks along the Thames
● Aerial view of the Palace of Westminster

TIPS

● It is best to book ahead, although not essential.
● Evening riders enjoy the London lights.
● Tickets include access to the 4-D Experience, a 3-D film with special effects.

Attracting 3.75 million visitors a year, London's most visible attraction, soaring 135m (443ft) above the South Bank of the Thames, affords spectacular city views.

Riding high Passengers ride in one of the 32 capsules that rotate smoothly through 360 degrees in a slow-moving 30-minute flight. Each capsule is fully enclosed and comfortably holds 25 people. Because the capsules are secured on the outside of the wheel (rather than hung from it like a Ferris Wheel), views through the large glass windows are totally unobstructed. Passengers can walk freely inside the capsules, which are kept level by a motor-ized motion stability system—although seating is provided. Each capsule is in touch with the ground via camera and radio links. The wheel is

Clockwise from far left: Opened in 2000, the Eye quickly became an established part of the South Bank's landscape; the Eye at night; the glass capsules, attached to the outside of the wheel, offer unobstructed views; an aerial view of the Palace of Westminster at dusk

in constant motion, revolving continuously at 0.26m (0.85ft) per second, a quarter of the average walking speed, enabling passengers to walk straight on and off the moving capsules. After dark, the trees lining the approach to the London Eye are bathed in magical blue lights, while the boarding platform appears to float on a cloud of more blue light.

Revolutionary design Conceived by David Marks and Julia Barfield to celebrate the millennium, the Eye represents the turning of the century and is a universal and ancient symbol of regeneration. It took seven years and the expertise of people from five European countries for their design to be realized. The Eye is on the riverside Thames Path, which continues east all the way to the Thames Barrier.

THE BASICS

www.londoneye.com

🔲 L7

✉ Riverside Gardens, next to County Hall, SE1

☎ 0870 990 8883; booking: 0871 781 3000;

🕐 Apr–Jun 10–9; Jul–Aug daily 10–9.30; Sep–Mar 10–8.30

🍴 Riverfront cafés

🚇 Waterloo, Westminster, Embankment, Charing Cross

🚆 Waterloo

♿ Very good. Boarding ramp available for wheelchair users

💷 Expensive

HIGHLIGHTS

- London Before London Gallery
- Hoard of 43 gold Roman coins
- Spitalfields Woman (Roman)
- Viking grave
- The lavish, late-18th-century Fanshawe dress
- Model of Tudor London
- Pleasure Gardens

A visit here is easily the best way to cruise through London's 2,000 years of history, pausing to see a Roman shoe or the Lord Mayor's State Coach, or to peek through a Victorian shop window; and it is even built on the West Gate of London's Roman fort.

A museum for London This is the world's largest and most comprehensive city museum, opened in 1976 in a building by Powell and Moya. The collection combines the old Guildhall Museum's City antiquities with the London Museum's costumes and other culturally related objects. The continuous building work and redevelopment in the City since the 1980s, allied with increased awareness about conservation, has ensured a steady flow of archaeological finds into the collection.

Clockwise from left: A window to the city's past: the lavish 18th-century Lord Mayor's State Coach on display at the museum; the original museum building, built in the 1970s; coins from the first century AD, part of the impressive Roman exhibit

A museum about London The building is, appropriately, in the barbican of the Roman fort, and the rooms are laid out chronologically to keep the story clear. The London Before London gallery follows the story of prehistoric Londoners before Roman settlement. One of the most impressive galleries is Roman London, which explains the founding of Londinium in about AD50 until AD410 when the Roman army quit Britain. The Expanding City chronicles the Great Fire of 1666 to the 1850s, an era of wealth, power and global influence. People make a city, so in every room it is Londoners who are really telling the story, whether it is through Roman ceramics or Tudor clothes. A £33 million redevelopment has resulted in superb displays and a mesmerizing re-creation of the 18th-century Vauxhall Pleasure Gardens.

THE BASICS

www.museumoflondon.org.uk

✚ P3

✉ 150 London Wall, EC2

☎ 020 7001 9844

🕐 Daily 10–6; galleries begin to close at 5.40. Closed 24–26 Dec

🍴 2 cafés

Ⓐ Barbican, Moorgate, St. Paul's

🚉 Moorgate

♿ Excellent

🎟 Free

❓ Full education schedule; audio tour

HIGHLIGHTS

- *Virgin Enthroned*, Cenni di Peppi Cimabue
- Cartoon, Leonardo da Vinci
- *Pope Julius II*, Raphael
- *The Arnolfini Wedding*, Van Eyck
- Equestrian portrait of Charles I by Van Dyck
- *The Haywain*, John Constable
- *Madonna of the Pinks*, Raphael
- *The Archers*, Henry Raeburn
- *Sunflowers*, Van Gogh
- *Mr and Mrs William Hallett*, Gainsborough
- *La Pointe de Hève*, Monet
- Restored entrance lobby and galleries

Here is a collection of very fine pictures—and for free, so you can drop in for a few minutes' peace in front of Leonardo da Vinci's cartoon in the Sainsbury Wing or Rubens's ravishing *Samson and Delilah*.

Quality collection Founded in 1824 with just 38 pictures, the National Gallery now has over 2,300 paintings, all on show. Spread throughout William Wilkins's neoclassical building and the Sainsbury Wing extension, they provide an extremely high-quality, concise panorama of European painting from Giotto to Cézanne.

Free from the start Unusual for a national painting collection, the nucleus is not royal but the collection of John Julius Angerstein, a self-made financier. From the start it was open to

Clockwise from far left: The gallery's impressive neoclassical facade, fronting Trafalgar Square; one of the elegant galleries in the East Wing; the East Wing of the National Gallery; a detail of Vincent van Gogh's 1888 painting Sunflowers; *the exterior of the museum*

all, free of charge, and provided a wide spectrum of British painting within a European context—aims that are still maintained today. However, there may be a charge for the temporary exhibitions in the Sainsbury Wing.

A first visit To take advantage of the rich artistic panorama, choose a room from each of the four chronologically arranged sections. Early paintings by Duccio di Buoninsegna, Jan van Eyck, Piero della Francesca and others fill the Sainsbury Wing. The West Wing has 16th-century pictures, including Michelangelo's *Entombment*, while the North Wing is devoted to 17th-century artists such as Van Dyck, Rubens, Rembrandt and painters of the Dutch school. The East Wing runs from Chardin through Gainsborough to Matisse and Picasso.

THE BASICS

www.nationalgallery.org.uk

➕ J6

✉ Trafalgar Square, WC2

☎ 020 7747 2885

🕐 Sat–Thu 10–6, Fri 10–9. Closed 24–26 Dec, 1 Jan

🍴 Brasserie, café

Ⓒ Charing Cross, Leicester Square

🚉 Charing Cross

♿ Excellent

💷 Free

❓ Guided tours (free daily 11.30 and 2.30, also Fri 7pm), lectures, films, audio guide, interactive screens. Free ten-minute talks (Mon–Fri 4pm), free lunchtime talks (Tue–Sat 1pm)

HIGHLIGHTS

- *Self-portrait with Barbara Hepworth*, Ben Nicholson
- Icon-like Richard II
- The Tudor Galleries
- *Queen Victoria*, Sir George Hayter
- *The Brontë Sisters*, by their brother, Branwell Brontë
- *Isambard Kingdom Brunel*, John Callcott
- *Sir Peter Hall*, Tom Phillips
- Using the self-guiding audio tour
- An unfinished sketch of Jane Austen (c.1810) by her sister, Cassandra

It's fascinating to see what someone famous looked like and how they chose to be painted—for instance, you would never expect Francis Drake to be dressed in red courtier's, rather than nautical clothes.

British record Founded in 1856 to collect portraits of the great and good in British life, and so inspire others to greatness, this is now the most comprehensive collection of its kind in the world, comprising watercolours, oil paintings, caricatures, silhouettes and photographs.

Start at the top The galleries, incorporating the Ondaatje Wing, are arranged chronologically, starting on the second floor—reached by stairs or elevator. Tudor monarchs kick off a visual *Who's Who* of British history that moves

Clockwise from far left: The main entrance to the National Portrait Gallery; the Tudor Galleries; portraits and busts from the Regency period on display in the acclaimed Weldon Galleries; an 1834 portrait of the Brontë sisters by their brother, Branwell; a mosaic at the museum entrance

through inventors, merchants, explorers and empire builders to modern politicians. Here you'll find Isambard K. Brunel, Robert Clive and Warren Hastings of India, Winston Churchill and Margaret Thatcher. There is Chaucer in his floppy hat, Kipling at his desk and A.A. Milne with his fictional creations Christopher Robin and Winnie-the-Pooh on his knee. Lesser-known sitters also merit a close look, such as the 18th-century portrait of the extensive Sharp Family, who formed an orchestra and played at Fulham every Sunday.

Modern times The Victorians insisted on entry only after death, but this rule has been revised. Among the many contemporary portraits, you may find those of footballer David Beckham, and ex-Beatle Sir Paul McCartney.

THE BASICS

www.npg.org.uk

➕ J5

✉ St. Martin's Place, WC2

☎ 020 7306 0055

🕐 Sat–Wed 10–6, Thu–Fri 10–9. Closed 24–26 Dec

🍴 Café, rooftop restaurant

Ⓜ Leicester Square, Charing Cross

🚆 Charing Cross

♿ Good

🎟 Free except for special exhibitions

❓ Lectures, events, explorer touchscreens

HIGHLIGHTS

- Giant Earth sculpture
- Dinosaur skeletons
- Fossilized frogs
- The Vault, a gallery of crystals, gems and meteorites
- Restless Surface Gallery
- Tank Room in the Darwin Centre

TIPS

- Use the side entrance on Exhibition Road.
- The museum is huge: Plan your visit carefully.

The museum building looks like a Romanesque cathedral and is wittily decorated with a zoo of animals to match its contents: extant animals on the west side, extinct ones on the east side.

Two museums in one Overflowing the British Museum, the Life Galleries were moved here in 1881. They tell the story of life on earth. The story of the earth itself is told in the Earth Galleries, beginning with a 300-million-year-old fossil of a fern. The Darwin Centre uses IT to make the most of the museum's 70 million objects and make the work of its 300 or so scientists accessible worldwide. Take the glass lift to its futuristic Cocoon building, then wend your way down its sloping walkways, taking in the exciting insect and plant displays.

Clockwise from far left: The museum's cavernous entrance hall; the escalator leading to the Red Zone, where galleries explore the nature of the Earth; insect specimens on display at Cocoon, part of the Darwin Centre; the original 1880 Waterhouse Building

Follow the zone Colour-coded zones help you plan your visit. In the Red Zone, dramatic sculptures and a giant metallic globe lead to galleries revealing how the planet has evolved: a treasury of minerals, gems and rocks; displays on how volcanoes and earthquakes happen; and the effect of man on nature. Exhibits in the Green Zone go from dinosaurs to birds and insects via fossils and our human ancestors. The Blue Zone celebrates the amazing diversity of our planet as it explores fish, amphibians and reptiles; investigates human biology; and gets up close to the blue whale, the largest creature on Earth. Don't miss the Images of Nature gallery, at the end of the Blue Zone, which houses a stunning collection of art inspired by nature. The superb Darwin Centre and quiet wildlife garden occupy the Orange Zone.

THE BASICS

www.nhm.ac.uk

🔳 B8

✉ Cromwell Road, SW7; also entrance on Exhibition Road

☎ 020 7942 5000

🕐 Daily 10–5.50. Closed 24–26 Dec

🍽 Meals, snacks, deli café, picnic areas

🚇 South Kensington

♿ Excellent

👆 Free; charge for some temporary exhibitions

❓ Regular tours, lectures, films, workshops

HIGHLIGHTS

● Red Lion Antiques Arcade, where it all began
● Spooky stuffed animals sold in Natural History
● The clocks and watches in Admiral Vernon arcade
● Arts and Crafts and art deco in the Crown Arcade

TIPS

● Saturday is by far the best day, when the antiques dealers set up stalls in the street.
● No price is totally fixed; bargain hard.
● It is true that the early bird finds the best prices.
● Join locals buying a treat at Tom's Delicatessen on Westbourne Grove.

Spend a Saturday wandering down Portobello Road, peering at the stalls and dipping into the shops behind them to seek out a special piece of china, a fascinating piece of glass or a pretty piece of jewellery.

Portobello Road Originally a lane leading down to Porto Bella Farm, this road has been a market site for over a century. Gypsies traded horses and herbs here in the 1870s, but the antiques dealers only arrived in the late 1940s. Today, Portobello Road Market claims to be the world's largest antiques market. It is really a series of markets that spill into surrounding streets where almost everything imaginable is sold. If you want a day-long party of fascination, fun and friendliness, come and take in the atmosphere.

Clockwise from left: Antiques arcades and galleries line Portobello Road; the Saturday-morning antiques market, when antiques traders and bargain-hunters crowd the area, sees Portobello Road at its busiest; fruit and vegetables are sold in the market's lower reaches

More than just stalls Starting at the top, there are the established specialist antiques shops for maps, silver, medals and collectables, where bargains are few. Don't miss Lipka Arcade and the 20th Century Theatre, opposite. Farther down, where the stalls begin, the stock is more varied and you can join locals in the pubs and cafés to discuss values and possible purchases. Here you'll find antique clothes, records and china next to contemporary ceramics and jewellery. Explore the by-roads, too.

For something different After the vegetable and organic food stalls you go under the Westway flyover and find restorative cafés. The tone changes. Here, look for funky bric-a-brac, cutting-edge street fashion, vintage clothes and even second-hand bicycles.

THE BASICS

www.portobelloroad.co.uk;
shopportobello.co.uk

➕ Off map at A5

✉ Market Office:
72 Tavistock Road, W11

🕐 Mon–Wed 9–6,
Thu 9–1, Fri–Sat 9–7.
Closed bank holidays

🚇 Notting Hill Gate,
Ladbroke Grove

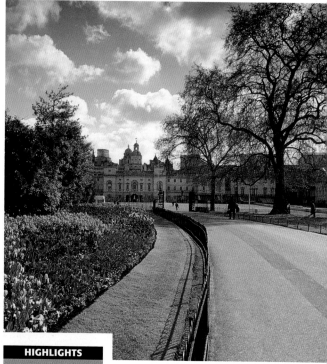

HIGHLIGHTS

- Springtime daffodils
- Whitehall views from the lake bridge
- Feeding the pelicans, daily 2.30–3.30
- Views to Buckingham Palace
- Exotic plants in the tropical border

TIPS

- Inn the Park café opens early and closes late.
- It's the perfect setting for summer picnics.
- Cyclists are welcome in the royal parks.

Drop in to St. James's Park to eat a sandwich and laze on a deckchair; try spotting palaces across the duck-filled lake or follow part of the Diana, Princess of Wales Memorial Walk.

Royal heart St. James's Park is the oldest and most royal of London's nine royal parks, surrounded by the Palace of Westminster, St. James's Palace, Buckingham Palace and the remains of Whitehall Palace. Kings and their courtiers have been frolicking here since 1536, when Henry VIII laid out a deer park in on what was then marshy water meadow and built a hunting lodge that became St. James's Palace. In the early 17th century, James I began the menagerie, including crocodiles and an elephant who drank a gallon of wine daily.

Left to right: With Buckingham Palace at its western end and the Houses of Parliament within easy reach, the park is a popular retreat for visitors; a drinking fountain; Springtime, when the daffodils are in bloom, is one of the best times to visit

French order In the mid-17th century, Charles II, influenced by Versailles, near Paris, redesigned the park to include a canal, Birdcage Walk (where he kept aviaries) and the gravelled Mall, where he played pell mell, a game similar to croquet. George IV, helped by John Nash and influenced by Humphrey Repton, softened the formal French lines into the English style in the 19th century, making this 37ha (93-acre) park of blossoming shrubs and curving paths popular with romantics.

Nature As the park is an important migration point and breeding area for birds, two full-time ornithologists look after up to 1,000 birds from more than 45 species. Pelicans live on Duck Island, a tradition begun when the Russian Ambassador gave some to Charles II.

THE BASICS

www.royalparks.org.uk

J7

The Mall, SW1

0300 061 2350

Daily 5am–midnight

Inn the Park (▷ 148)

St. James's Park, Green Park, Westminster

Victoria

Very good

Free

Changing the Guard (on Horseguards Parade). Bird talks; guided walks

HIGHLIGHTS

- Sung evensong
- Frescoes and mosaics
- Wren's Great Model in the Triforium (upstairs)
- Triple-layered dome weighing 76,000 tons
- Jean Tijou's wrought-iron sanctuary gates
- Wellington's memorial
- *Light of the World*, Holman Hunt
- The view across London
- Wren's epitaph under the dome

To slip into St. Paul's for evensong, and sit gazing up at the mosaics as the choir's voices soar, is to enjoy a moment of absolute peace and beauty. Go early or late to avoid the crowds.

Wren's London After the restoration of the monarchy in 1660, artistic patronage bloomed under Charles II. Following the Great Fire of London in 1666, which destroyed four-fifths of the City, Christopher Wren took main stage as King's Surveyor-General. The spires and steeples of his 51 churches, of which 23 still stand, surrounded his masterpiece, St. Paul's.

The fourth St. Paul's This cathedral church for the diocese of London was founded in AD604 by King Ethelbert of Kent. The first three

Clockwise from far left: The view of St. Paul's Cathedral from Festival Gardens; the interior of the magnificent dome, decorated with frescoes by Sir James Thornhill; the choir stalls and high altar; St. Paul's before the Fire of London in 1666; architect Sir Christopher Wren

West View of St. Pauls Cathedral before the Fire of London.

churches burned down. Wren's, built in stone and paid for with a special coal tax, was the first English cathedral built by a single architect, the only one with a dome, and the only one in the English baroque style. A £40 million cleaning-and-repair project marked the cathedral's 300th anniversary in 2010. Statues and memorials of Britain's famous crowd the interior and crypt—heroes Wellington and Nelson, artists Turner and Reynolds, as well as Wren himself.

The climb The 528 steps to the Golden Gallery at the top are worth the effort. Shallow steps rise to the Whispering Gallery for views of Sir James Thornhill's dome, decorated with frescoes and 19th-century mosaics. For virtual access to the dome, visit Oculus, a 270-degree film experience in the crypt.

THE BASICS

www.stpauls.co.uk

➕ N4

✉ Ludgate Hill, EC4

☎ 020 7246 8350

🕐 Mon–Sat 8.30–4. Galleries and Oculus: 9.30–4.15. Services include Mon–Sat 5, Sun 8, 11, 3.15, 6

🍴 Restaurant, café

Ⓢ St. Paul's

🚆 City Thameslink

♿ Very good

💷 Expensive

❓ Multimedia, audio and guided tours included; organ recitals

Even if you are no scientist, it's thrilling to understand how a plane flies, how Newton's reflecting telescope worked, or how we receive satellite television. You'll find the answers using interactive exhibits. This is science at its most accessible.

Industry and science Opened in 1857, this museum comes closest to fulfilling Prince Albert's educational aims when he founded the South Kensington Museums after the Great Exhibition of 1851. Its full title is the National Museum of Science and Industry. Over the seven floors, which contain more than 60 collections, the story of human industry, discovery and invention is recounted through various tools and products, from exquisite Georgian cabinets to a satellite launcher.

Clockwise from far left: Landmark designs are displayed in the Making the Modern World gallery; displays in the Who Am I? gallery explore the wonders of human genetics and intelligence; one of the child-friendly exhibits in the Launchpad; an early 20th-century engine in the Energy Hall

Science made fun See how vital everyday objects were invented and then developed for use in Making the Modern World; find out what makes you smarter than a chimp in Who Am I?; and get involved in the very latest scientific hot topics in Antenna. The galleries vary from rooms of beautiful 18th-century objects to an astronaut's moon capsule and in-depth explanations of abstract concepts. You can even learn the basic principles of flying by testing out the hands-on equipment in the Flight gallery. Health Matters reveals how technology has dramatically changed medicine. The interactive Challenge of Materials and the high-tech Launch Pad, a favourite with children, explore science, technology and the complex world, while the Atmosphere gallery tackles climate science brilliantly.

THE BASICS

www.sciencemuseum.
org.uk
⊞ C8
⊠ Exhibition Road, SW7
☎ 0870 870 4868
🕐 Daily 10–6
🍴 Restaurants, cafés, picnic area in basement
🚇 South Kensington
♿ Excellent (tel helpline 020 7942 4000)
🎟 Free; IMAX cinema expensive
❓ Guided tours, demonstrations, historic characters, lectures, films, workshops

HIGHLIGHTS

- Guided tour storytellers
- Attending a performance
- Interactive displays
- Costume collection

TIP

- Tours and performances take place in all weathers, so dress appropriately.

A faithful reconstruction of The Bard's open-air theatre, where Shakespeare's plays are performed and cutting-edge new writers have the opportunity to shine.

One man's vision From his first visit to London in 1949, actor and director Sam Wanamaker dreamed of recreating Shakespeare's 16th-century Globe theatre as close as possible to its original site by the Thames at Bankside. Several decades and a long struggle later, the theatre opened in 1997 with a production of *Henry V*.

Tradition to the core Constructed of English oak with mortise-and tenon-joints, lime plaster and water reed thatch roof (the first permitted since the Great Fire of London in 1666), the building techniques used were painstakingly

Left: watching a play here gives you a unique insight into Elizabethan theatre; below: The Globe has been reconstructed on London's Bankside, a short distance from the site of the original building that hosted Shakespeare's plays

THE BASICS

www.shakespearesglobe.com

🚲 P6

✉ 21 New Globe Walk, SE1

☎ Exhibition and tour office 020 7902 1500 Theatre Box Office 020 7401 9919

🕐 Exhibition daily 9–5.30; tours daily, check website for times. Main stage performance season mid-Apr to mid-Oct

🍴 Restaurant, bar, café

Ⓤ Blackfriars, Mansion House, London Bridge, Southwark

🚆 London Bridge

⛴ Bankside Pier

♿ Good. Access information line tel: 020 7902 1409

💷 Expensive (incl guided theatre tour and exhibition audio guide)

❓ Temporary exhibitions, full educational schedule

accurate. Its thrust stage projects into a large circular yard surrounded by three tiers of simple benches (cushions can be hired) for 857 people. Only the seating area and stage are covered, so the 700 'groundlings' standing in the yard below the stage swelter in the heat and get very wet when it rains. An exhibition beneath the theatre tells its history and explores the London Shakespeare would have known.

New theatre A £7.5-million indoor Jacobean theatre, the Sam Wanamaker Playhouse, has created an intimate, year-round theatrical experience, quite different from that of the Globe. Performing the plays of Shakespeare and his contemporaries in the surroundings for which they were originally intended, it seats 340 people and is predominantly lit by candles.

● *The Rake's Progress, The Election*, Hogarth
● Sarcophagus of Seti I
● Sir Thomas Lawrence's portrait of Soane
● Canaletto's paintings

TIPS

● The museum is not suitable for children.
● Atmospheric candlelit evening openings are held monthly.
● Tours are on Saturday at 11am (inexpensive).

As you move about the gloriously over-furnished rooms of Soane's two houses and into the calm upstairs drawing room, his presence is so strong and his genius so pervasive that you feel you would not be surprised if he were there to greet you.

The architect This double treasure-house in leafy Lincoln's Inn Fields, central London's largest square, is where the neoclassical architect Sir John Soane lived. First he designed No. 12 and lived there from 1792. Then he bought No. 13 next door, rebuilt it with cunningly proportioned rooms, and lived there from 1813 until his death in 1837. Meanwhile, he also designed Holy Trinity church on Marylebone Road (1824–48), and parts of the Treasury, Whitehall. His model for his

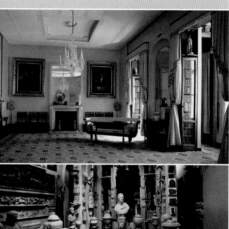

Clockwise from far left: Sir John Soane remodelled two adjoining houses to create his home in Lincoln's Inn Fields; the Breakfast Room, hung with three paintings by Canaletto, are among the museum's treasures; one of the first-floor entertaining rooms; part of Soane's eclectic collection

masterpiece, the (destroyed) Bank of England, is here (recreated rooms now form part of the bank's museum, ▷ 66). No. 14 is now an area for Adam Studies.

The collector Soane was an avid collector. He found that every art object could inspire his work, so his rooms were a visual reference library. Hogarth's paintings unfold from the walls in layers. There are so many sculptures, paintings and antiquities that unless you keep your eyes peeled you are likely to miss a Watteau drawing or something better.

Opening up the Soane The project to restore the museum to its appearance at the time of Sir John's death is ongoing, with all the works scheduled for completion in 2016.

THE BASICS

www.soane.org

➕ L4

✉ 13 Lincoln's Inn Fields, WC2

☎ 020 7405 2107

🕐 Tue–Sat 10–5 (also first Tue of month 6–9pm). Closed 24–26 Dec, 1 Jan, Sun, Mon and bank hols

🚇 Holborn, Chancery Lane

🚉 Farringdon

♿ Call in advance

💵 Free (donation)

❓ Free audio tours on website

HIGHLIGHTS

- Courtauld Collection
- The Fridart Collection
- *A Bar at the Folies-Bergère*, Manet
- Rubens paintings
- *The Trinity*, Botticelli

Somerset House was transformed from a lavish but forgotten building into a riverside palace. Spend some time here and enjoy French Impressionist masterpieces, summer concerts and dancing fountains.

Palatial home A majestic triple-arch gateway leads from the Strand into Sir William Chambers' English Palladian government offices (1776–86). The Courtauld Collection is housed in rooms lavishly decorated for the Royal Academy, before its move to Piccadilly. Ahead, the great courtyard has fountains, a theatre, an ice-rink and café tables, according to the season. A superb fine dining restaurant on the summer terrace, with sweeping Thames views, is a seasonal treat. Changing exhibitions are held in the Embankment Galleries.

Clockwise from far left: The courtyard of Somerset House; artistic treasures on display in the Courtauld Gallery; the Courtauld's lavishly decorated rooms, which were originally used by the Royal Academy; the elegant staircase leading to the upper floors of the Courtauld Gallery

Courtauld Gallery Industrialist Samuel Courtauld's collection of French Impressionist and post-Impressionist paintings, with works by Renoir, Cézanne, Van Gogh, Manet, Seurat and Gauguin, are on display. There are also 18th-century portraits by Goya and Gainsborough; canvases and sketches by Rubens; works by Botticelli and Tintoretto; and an important Gothic and medieval collection. Twentieth-century highlights include works by Matisse, Dufy, Kandinsky and the Bloomsbury group.

Drawings, prints and sculpture The excellent collection of prints includes works by Michelangelo, Dürer and Leonardo da Vinci, while its sculpture collection spans antiquity to the 20th century. The decorative arts are represented by fine Islamic ceramics and metalwork.

THE BASICS

www.somersethouse.org.uk

+ L5

✉ Somerset House, Strand, WC2

☎ 020 7845 4600

🕐 Daily 10–6; extended hours for Courtyard, River Terrace and restaurant

🍴 Cafés, restaurant

Ⓣ Temple

🚆 Blackfriars, Charing Cross

♿ Excellent

💷 Somerset House free; Courtauld Gallery moderate

❓ Free guided tours of Somerset House Thu 1.15, 2.45, Sat 12.15, 1.15, 2.15 and 3.15. Tickets available from 10.30am from the information desk in the Seaman's Hall, South Building

HIGHLIGHTS

- The Clore Gallery
- Thomas Gainsborough portrait
- *Flatford Mill*, Constable
- A William Blake vision
- A William Hogarth caricature
- A Barbara Hepworth stone or wood sculpture
- A work on paper by David Hockney
- *The Opening of Waterloo Bridge*, Constable
- Temporary exhibitions
- The Tate to Tate ferry

Moving through the galleries past Gainsborough portraits, Turner landscapes and Hepworth sculptures, this is an intimate social history of Britain told by its artists.

The Gallery The Tate Gallery was opened in 1897, named after the millionaire Henry Tate, who paid for the core building and donated his Victorian pictures to it. The national collection, renamed Tate Britain after the modern art collection was moved to Tate Modern (▷ 54–55), remained in the original building on Millbank.

The Millbank Project This is a 20-year program of building works designed to transform the gallery. The first part, finished in 2013, upgraded the Millbank Entrance, Rotunda and some of the galleries.

Clockwise from far left: The imposing Millbank entrance to Tate Britain; paintings on display in the gallery; the rotunda dome, a masterpiece of Victorian architecture; the Turner Collection, the largest collection of works by J.M.W. Turner in the world, is housed in the modern Clore Gallery

British art The galleries are helpfully divided into four chronological suites. You can follow the visual story of British art from 1500 until the present day. Although paintings, sculptures, installations and works in other media are changed regularly, you may well see Van Dyck's lavish portraits of the 17th-century British aristocracy, William Hogarth's prints and richly coloured Pre-Raphaelite canvases. Do not miss the great Turner collection housed in the adjoining Clore Gallery.

Turner Prize Britain's most prestigious and controversial prize to celebrate young British talent is run by the Tate and awarded each autumn. Founded in 1984, winners have included Damien Hurst, Grayson Perry and Chris Ofili.

THE BASICS

www.tate.org.uk

🔢 J9

✉ Millbank, SW1; entrances on Millbank and Atterbury Street

☎ 020 7887 8888

🕙 Daily 10–6.

🍴 Restaurant, café

Ⓜ Pimlico, Vauxhall, Westminster

🚆 Victoria

♿ Very good

🎫 Free except for special exhibitions

ℹ Full education schedule; audio tours

HIGHLIGHTS
Although diplays change, look out for works by:
● Pablo Picasso
● Claude Monet
● Henri Matisse
● Constantin Brancusi
● Jackson Pollock
● Mark Rothko
● Bridget Riley
● Marcel Duchamp
● Andy Warhol

The national collection of modern art fills the magnificent spaces of George Gilbert Scott's monumental Bankside Power Station by the Thames, making it a radical focus for the long strip of riverside arts emporia.

World-class art On a par with the Metropolitan Museum of Modern Art in New York, the collection that once shared space with the Tate's British collection (▷ 52–53) now blossoms in its own huge spaces. Swiss architects Herzog & de Meuron have created an exciting contemporary structure within the handsome brick building, making it ideal for exhibiting large-scale works of art in an innovative way. Gallery events, cafés, a big shop and a rooftop restaurant complete the total package for a great day on the South Bank or, using the

Clockwise from far left: The monumental Turbine Hall, used for temporary exhibitions; the Millennium Bridge, linking Tate Modern with the City; a computer-generated image of the new extension to Tate Modern; The Kiss (1901–04) by Auguste Rodin; Claude Monet's Water-Lilies (c.1916)

Millennium Bridge designed by Caro and Rogers, in combination with City sightseeing.

20th century and more The most influential artists of the 20th century are all represented, including Picasso, Matisse, Dalí, Duchamp, Rodin, Klee and Warhol—as well as British artists such as Bacon, Hepworth, Hockney and Nicholson. Together they represent all the major periods and movements in 20th-century art. Suites of rooms, each devoted to one subject, mix together pieces from various periods.

Tate Modern project A striking new building rising behind the power station will transform the galleries. With 11 levels, it will double the space for displaying the collection and for installation and performance art.

THE BASICS

www.tate.org.uk

⊞ N6

✉ Bankside, SE1

☎ 020 7887 8888

🕐 Sun–Thu 10–6, Fri–Sat 10–10. Closed 24–26 Dec

🍴 Cafés, restaurant

🚇 Blackfriars, Southwark

🚉 Blackfriars, London Bridge

♿ Very good

🎫 Free, charge for some special exhibitions

❓ Full educational schedule. Choice of free daily audio tours

HIGHLIGHTS

- Lambeth Palace
- Houses of Parliament
- London Eye
- St. Paul's Cathedral
- Tower Bridge
- Tower of London
- Thames Barrier

TIPS

- Shop around for the best deals.
- The Tate Boat plies between the two galleries.
- Take a jacket; London weather changes quickly.

A cruise along the Thames is a leisurely way to see the city. It gives a new perspective to London's development and history, which is inextricably linked with this great river.

Wonderful sights Many companies run river cruises and water-buses on the river. A particularly good stretch is from Westminster Pier in an easterly direction, which takes in a host of sights. This marks the point where the river enters central London and becomes a working highway, until recently lined with shipping, docks and warehouses. At this point the Thames flows between Lambeth Palace and the Houses of Parliament (▷ 22–23) and past the London Eye (▷ 28–29) and the Southbank Centre, making a northern loop past the Victoria Embankment and towards the Millennium

Clockwise from top left: A view over the Thames to St. Paul's Cathedral and the high-rises of the City; amphibious craft (DUKWs) provide tours with a difference (see panel, page 167); the landmark Tower Bridge; Big Ben and the Houses of Parliament; the Thames Flood Barrier

Bridge, linking St. Paul's Cathedral (▷ 42–43) and Tate Modern (▷ 54–55).

Great bridges Beyond Shakespeare's Globe (▷ 46–47) and Southwark Cathedral (▷ 74) the river reaches London Bridge, the modern crossing that replaced the 1831 version, itself replacing its arched medieval predecessor. The next crossing is Tower Bridge, designed to allow tall ships passage between the city and the sea. On the north bank is the Tower of London (▷ 58–59), William the Conqueror's fort placed strategically to protect the port.

Modern versus maritime From here the river passes the redeveloped Docklands. Seafaring is the theme as the Thames reaches Greenwich (▷ 20–21) and then the Thames Barrier.

THE BASICS

➕ K7

✉ Start point: Westminster Pier

Ⓜ Westminster

🚢 **Circular Cruise Westminster**

✉ 020 7936 2033; www.crownrivercruise. co.uk

City Cruises

✉ 020 7740 0400; www.citycruises.com

Thames River Services

020 7930 4097; www. westminsterpier.co.uk

Westminster Passenger Service Association

✉ 020 7930 2062; www.wpsa.co.uk

💷 Moderate to expensive

HIGHLIGHTS

- Medieval Palace
- Raleigh's room
- Imperial State Crown
- Tower ravens
- Grand Punch Bowl, 1829
- St. John's Chapel

TIPS

- For advance tickets call 0844 482 7799 (44 20 3166 6000 from outside the UK). Alternatively, buy them online at www.hrp.org.uk.
- If buying tickets on the day, it's vital to arrive early to avoid lines.

The superbly restored rooms of Edward I's 13th-century palace bring the Tower alive as the royal palace and place of pageantry it was. Don't miss gazing at the Crown Jewels.

Medieval glory The Tower of London is Britain's best medieval fortress. William the Conqueror (1066–87) began it as a show of brute force and Edward I (1272–1307) completed it. William's Caen stone White Tower, built within old Roman walls, was an excellent defence: It was 27m (90ft) high, with walls 4.5m (15ft) thick, and space for soldiers, servants and nobles. Henry III began the Inner Wall, the moat, his own watergate—and the royal zoo. Edward I built the Outer Wall, several towers and Traitor's Gate, and moved the Mint and Crown Jewels here.

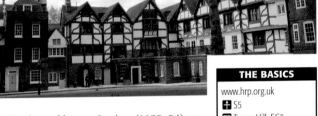

Clockwise from far left: The mighty White Tower, begun by William the Conqueror in 1078; Waterloo Block, where the Crown Jewels are on display; Yeoman Warders (more commonly known as Beefeaters), historically guardians of the Tower; Tower Green, former scene of private executions

Wonder and horror Stephen (1135–54) was the first king to live here, James I (1603–25) the last. From here Edward I went in procession to his coronation and Henry VIII paraded through the city bedecked in cloth of gold. The Barons seized the Tower to force King John to put his seal to the Magna Carta in 1215; and two princes were murdered while their uncle was being crowned Richard III. Since 1485 it has been guarded by Yeoman Warders or 'Beefeaters', who also now give guided tours.

Centuries of history The Tower has been a palace, fortress, state prison and execution site and its gates are still locked every night. If the history is overwhelming there is help: a good welcome area, jolly guided tours, a serious audio tour and numerous interactive displays.

THE BASICS

www.hrp.org.uk

⊞ S5

✉ Tower Hill, EC3

☎ 0844 482 7777

🕐 Mar–Oct Tue–Sat 9–5.30, Sun–Mon 10–5.30; Nov–Feb Tue–Sat 9–4.30, Sun–Mon 10–4.30

🍴 Cafés, restaurant

Ⓜ Tower Hill

🚆 Fenchurch Street, London Bridge, Docklands Light Railway (Tower Gateway)

♿ Excellent for Jewel House

💷 Expensive

❓ Free guided tours every 30 min; audio tours

HIGHLIGHTS

● British Galleries
● India and Islamic Galleries
● Jewellery Gallery
● Glass Gallery
● Leonardo da Vinci notebooks
● Silver collection
● Raphael Gallery
● Architecture Gallery
● The Hereford Screen

TIPS

● Hang out in the courtyard.
● Join a gallery tour or talk.
● Evening openings have a good atmosphere.

Part of the Victoria and Albert Museum's glory is that each room is unexpected; it may contain a French boudoir, plaster casts of classical sculptures, antique silver or exquisite contemporary glass.

A vision The V&A started as the South Kensington Museum. It was Prince Albert's vision: arts and science objects available to all people to inspire them to invent and create, with the accent on commercial design and craftsmanship. Since it opened in 1857, its collection, now comprising over a million works, has become so encyclopaedic, it ranks as the world's largest decorative arts museum.

Bigger and bigger Its size is unmanageable: 11km (7 miles) of gallery space on six floors.

Clockwise from left: The V&A, which opened in 1857, now ranks as the world's largest museum of decorative arts; exhibits in the museum's The Renaissance City 1350–1600 display; the Jameel Gallery, where exhibits showcase Islamic art from the eighth and ninth centuries

Its content is even more so: barely five per cent of the 44,000 objects in the Indian department are on show. Larger museum objects include whole London house facades, grand rooms and the Raphael Cartoons. Despite this, contemporary work has been energetically bought: more than 60 per cent of furniture entering the museum is 20th century.

Riches and rags Not every object in the museum is precious: there are everyday things, unique pieces and opportunities to discover a fascination for a new subject—perhaps lace, ironwork, tiles or Japanese textiles. See the lavishly refurbished British and Whiteley Silver galleries, the magnificent collections in the Medieval and Renaissance Galleries and the striking new Ceramics Gallery and Study Centre.

THE BASICS

www.vam.ac.uk

✚ C8

✉ Cromwell Road, SW7

☎ 020 7942 2000

🕐 Daily 10–5.45 (Fri 10–10)

🍴 Restaurant, café

Ⓢ South Kensington

♿ Very good

🎫 Free (except some special exhibitions)

❓ Free daily guided, introductory tours. Talks, courses, demonstrations, workshops and concerts

HIGHLIGHTS

- Poets' Corner
- Sir Isaac Newton memorial
- Sir James Thornhill's window
- Henry VII's Chapel
- Edward the Confessor's Chapel
- St. Faith's Chapel
- Grave of the Unknown Soldier
- Little Cloister and College Garden
- Weekday sung evensong at 5pm

TIPS

- Attend a service and hear the choirboys, accompanied by the abbey organ.
- Free organ recitals, Sun 5.45; Summer organ festival (mid-Jul to mid-Aug).

The best time to be in the abbey is for the 8am service, sometimes held in St. Faith's Chapel. Follow this with a wander in the nave and cloisters before the crowds arrive.

The kernel of London's second city It was Edward the Confessor who in the 11th century began the rebuilding of the Benedictine abbey church of St. Peter, which was consecrated in 1065. The first sovereign to be crowned there was William the Conqueror in 1066. Successive kings were patrons, as were the pilgrims who flocked to the Confessor's shrine. Henry III (1216–72) employed Master Henry de Reyns to begin the Gothic abbey that stands today, and Henry VII (1485–1509) built his Tudor chapel with its delicate fan vaulting. Since William I, all sovereigns have been crowned

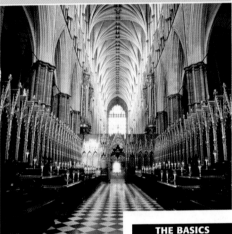

Clockwise from far left: The West Front; the Grave of the Unknown Soldier, adorned with Remembrance Day poppies; the shrine of Edward the Confessor, the abbey's founder; the choir stalls and ornate gilt altar; the abbey's magnificent vaulted ceiling

here—even after Henry VIII broke with Rome in 1533; and all were buried here up to George II (after which Windsor became the royal burial place, ▷ 79). It has also hosted 16 royal marriages, most recently that of Prince William and Catherine Middleton in 2011.

Daunting riches The abbey is massive, full of monuments and very popular. From the nave's west end enjoy the view of the abbey, then look over the Victorian Gothic choir screen into Henry V's chantry. Having explored the chapels, the royal necropolis and Poets' Corner, leave time for the quiet cloister with superb views of the flying buttresses supporting the nave. In the abbey museum you can see macabre wax effigies, including those of Queen Elizabeth I and Lord Nelson, and a 13th-century altarpiece.

THE BASICS

www.westminster-abbey.org

✚ J8

✉ Broad Sanctuary, SW1; entry by North Door

☎ 020 7222 5152

🕐 Abbey: Mon–Sat times vary, call or check website; no photography. Abbey Museum, College Garden: daily various hours. Closed before special services, Sun, 24–25 Dec, Good Fri and Commonwealth Day

🚇 Westminster, St. James's Park

🚆 Victoria

♿ Good

💷 Expensive

❓ Guided tours, audio guides

More to See

This section contains other great places to visit if you have more time. Some are in the heart of the city while others are a short journey away, found under Further Afield. This chapter also has fantastic excursions that you should set aside a whole day to visit.

MORE TO SEE

In the Heart of the City

30 ST. MARY AXE
This landmark tower, designed by Foster & Partners and affectionately known as 'The Gherkin', adds wit to the cluster of tall buildings in London's financial hub.
✚ R4 ⊠ 30 St. Mary Axe, EC3 ⊙ Not open to the general public 🚇 Bank

ALBERT MEMORIAL
www.royalparks.org.uk
George Gilbert Scott's Gothic extravaganza dedicated to Prince Albert, celebrates Victorian achievement, with marble statues representing the Arts, Sciences, Industry and Continents. The finely carved frieze at its base depicts famous people in the Arts.
✚ B7 ⊠ Alexandra Gate, Kensington Gardens, SW7 🚇 South Kensington

ALL-HALLOWS-BY-THE-TOWER
www.allhallowsbythetower.org.uk
Founded in AD675, the church has a Saxon arch, a Roman pavement, a carving by Grinling Gibbons and the Crypt Museum.
✚ R5 ⊠ Byward Street, EC3 ☎ 020 7481 2928 ⊙ Church: Mon–Fri 8–6, Sat 10–5

Sun 10–1 except during services. Closed public hols 🚇 Tower Hill 💷 Free

APSLEY HOUSE (WELLINGTON MUSEUM)
www.english-heritage.org.uk
The splendid mansion was built for Arthur Wellesley, Duke of Wellington (1769–1852). The sumptuous interior houses his magnificent collection of paintings and decorative arts, with works by Velázquez and Rubens, as well as silver, porcelain and Canova's nude statue of Napoleon.
✚ F7 ⊠ Hyde Park Corner, W1 ☎ 020 7499 5676 ⊙ Apr–Oct Wed–Sun 11–5; Nov–Mar 11–4 (Apsley House closed for refurbishment Nov 13–Mar 14) 🚇 Hyde Park Corner 💷 Moderate

BANK OF ENGLAND MUSEUM
www.bankofengland.co.uk/museum
Exhibits illustrate the history of Britain's monetary and banking system since 1694. Take time to appreciate the re-creations of Soane's rooms, and Sir Herbert Baker's Rotunda. The museum stages changing exhibitions.

The glittering Albert Memorial and nearby Albert Hall

30 St. Mary Axe, dubbed 'The Gherkin'

➕ Q4 ✉ Bartholomew Lane, EC2 ☎ 020 7601 5545 ⏰ Mon–Fri 10–5, last entry 4.45 🚇 Bank 💷 Free

BENJAMIN FRANKLIN HOUSE

www.benjaminfranklinhouse.org

The Founding Father of the United States lived at this address for 15 years in the 18th century. His life as an inventor and philosopher is revealed through the innovative Historical Experience shows.

➕ K6 ✉ 36 Craven Street, WC2 ☎ 020 7839 2006 ⏰ Wed–Sun 12–5, last tour 4.15 🚇 Charing Cross 💷 Moderate

BOROUGH MARKET

www.boroughmarket.org.uk

Stallholders, many artisan producers, sell their goods at London's most exciting food market.

➕ Q6 ✉ Southwark Street, SE1 ⏰ Thu 11–5, Fri 12–6, Sat 8–5 🚇 London Bridge 🚇 London Bridge

BRITISH LIBRARY

www.bl.uk

Colin St. John Wilson's 1998 red-brick building houses the nation's books and manuscripts, with public galleries and a piazza. It holds interesting exhibitions on different aspects of the library's collection.

➕ J1 ✉ 96 Euston Road, NW1 ☎ 0843 208 1144 ⏰ Mon–Fri 9.30–6, Tue 9.30–8, Sat 9.30–5, Sun 11–5 🍴 Café, restaurant 🚇 King's Cross 💷 Donation

BROMPTON ORATORY

www.bromptonoratory.com

Standing next door to the V&A, the flamboyant Oratory of St. Philip Neri was built in 1884 and given a sumptuous, sculpture-filled interior.

➕ C8 ✉ Brompton Road, SW7 ☎ 020 7808 0900 ⏰ Daily 6.30am–8pm 🚇 South Kensington 💷 Donation

CHARLES DICKENS MUSEUM

www.dickensmuseum.com

Visit the house where Dickens wrote novels *Nicholas Nickleby* and *Oliver Twist*. A £3.1 million restoration project has given visitors a real sense of his life and work.

➕ L2 ✉ 48 Doughty Street, WC1 ☎ 020 7405 2127 ⏰ Daily 10–5, last admission 4 🚇 Russell Square 💷 Moderate

Fresh shellfish at Borough Market

The British Library piazza, with Eduardo Paolozzi's bronze statue

CHRISTCHURCH SPITALFIELDS

www.christchurchspitalfields.org

Nicholas Hawksmoor's 1729 masterpiece has been finely restored and is often used for concerts.

⊞ S3 ✉ Fournier Street, E1 ☎ 020 7377 6793 🕙 Tue 11–4, Sun 1–4 🚇 Liverpool Street 🎫 Donation

CHURCHILL WAR ROOMS

www.iwm.org.uk

Churchill directed Britain's war effort from these secret rooms, evocatively kept as they were in 1945. Exhibits in the Churchill Museum tell of his life and times.

⊞ J7 ✉ Clive Steps, King Charles Street, SW1 ☎ 020 7930 6961 🕙 Daily 9.30–6 (last admission 5) 🚇 St. James's Park, Westminster 🎫 Expensive

CITY HALL

www.london.gov.uk

Architect Sir Norman Foster's distinctive glass building is home to the Mayor of London and the Greater London Authority.

⊞ R6 ✉ The Queen's Walk, SE1 ☎ 020 7983 4000 🕙 Mon–Thu 8.30–6, Fri 8.30–5.30 🚇 London Bridge 🎫 Free

CLARENCE HOUSE

www.royal.gov.uk

Built for Prince William, Duke of Clarence and later William IV, this was the late Queen Mother's London home, now renovated by its current resident, the Prince of Wales. Five rooms used by Prince Charles and the Duchess of Cornwall for official engagements can be seen. All tickets are timed and must be prebooked.

⊞ H7 ✉ Off the Mall, SW1 ☎ 020 7766 7303 🕙 Aug Mon–Fri 10–4, Sat–Sun 10–5.30 🚇 St. James's Park, Green Park 🎫 Moderate

CLEOPATRA'S NEEDLE

The 26m (86ft) pink granite obelisk was made in Egypt in 1450BC and records the triumphs of Rameses the Great.

⊞ K6 ✉ Victoria Embankment, WC2 🚇 Embankment, Charing Cross 🎫 Free

CLOCKMAKERS' MUSEUM

www.clockmakers.org

This collection of exquisite timepieces tick-tocking away includes Thomas Tompion masterpieces.

City Hall, home to the Greater London Authority

🚇 P4 ✉ Guildhall Library, Aldermanbury, EC2 ☎ 020 7332 1870 🕐 Mon–Sat 9.30–4.45 🚇 St. Paul's, Bank 💷 Free

COVENT GARDEN PIAZZA

www.coventgardenlondonuk.com
London's first square was laid out in the 1630s by architect Inigo Jones. It later became a fruit and vegetable market. Redeveloped in the 1980s, the piazza became a popular meeting and eating place, with lively street entertainment.
🚇 K5 🚇 Covent Garden

DR. JOHNSON'S HOUSE

www.drjohnsonshouse.org
Dr. Samuel Johnson lived here between 1748 and 1759 while compiling his famous dictionary.
🚇 M4 ✉ 17 Gough Square, EC4 ☎ 020 7353 3745 🕐 May–Sep Mon–Sat 11–5.30; Oct–Apr Mon–Sat 11–5 🚇 Chancery Lane, Temple, Holborn 🚉 Blackfriars
💷 Inexpensive

EROS

Alfred Gilbert's memorial (1893) to the philanthropic 7th Earl of Shaftesbury (1801–85), *The Angel of Christian Charity*, is popularly referred to as Eros, although it actually depicts Anteros, the god of selfless love.
🚇 H5 ✉ Piccadilly Circus, W1
🚇 Piccadilly Circus

FOUNDLING MUSEUM

www.foundlingmuseum.org.uk
When Thomas Coran founded a hospice for abandoned children in 1739, Handel and Hogarth helped to raise funds. Both the building and the art are magnificent.
🚇 K2 ✉ 40 Brunswick Square, WC1 ☎ 020 7841 3600 🕐 Tue–Sat 10–5, Sun 11–5 🚇 Russell Square 💷 Moderate

GARDEN MUSEUM

www.gardenmuseum.org.uk
Celebrating the plant-hunting Tradescants and 400 years of garden and plant history in an abandoned church, knot garden and gallery.
🚇 L8 ✉ Lambeth Palace Road, SE1 ☎ 020 7401 8865 🕐 Daily 10.30–5 (Sat 4), closed 1st Mon in month 🍴 Café 🚇 Lambeth North
💷 Moderate

A street performer entertains the crowds at Covent Garden Piazza

Eros, at the heart of Piccadilly Circus

GOLDEN HINDE II

www.goldenhinde.com

The ship is an exact replica of the 16th-century galleon in which Sir Francis Drake circumnavigated the globe. Take a look at the website for events and tours.

➕ Q6 ✉ St. Mary Overie Dock, Cathedral Street, SE1 ☎ 020 7403 0123 🕐 Usually daily 10–5.30, but hours vary 🚇 London Bridge 🚉 London Bridge 💷 Moderate

GREEN PARK

www.royalparks.org.uk

Covering 19ha (47 acres), Green Park is famous for its mature trees, tree-lined avenues and spring daffodils.

➕ G7 ✉ SW1 ☎ 0300 061 2350 🕐 Daily 24 hrs 🚇 Green Park, Hyde Park Corner 💷 Free

GUILDHALL ART GALLERY

www.city of london.gov.uk

The gallery offers two remarkable things to see: the Guildhall's quirky collection of mostly British pictures, and part of Roman London's huge amphitheatre, built in AD200 and rediscovered in 1988.

➕ P4 ✉ Guildhall Yard, Gresham Street, EC2 ☎ 020 7332 3700 🕐 Mon–Sat 10–5, Sun 12–4 🚇 St. Paul's, Bank 💷 Free

HANDEL HOUSE MUSEUM

www.handelhouse.org

Anyone who plays an instrument or sings *The Messiah* should visit the composer's London home from 1723 until 1759. There are weekly concerts and events.

➕ G5 ✉ 25 Brook Street, W1 ☎ 020 7495 1685 🕐 Tue–Wed, Fri–Sat 10–6, Thu 10–8, Sun 12–6 🚇 Bond Street 💷 Moderate

HAYWARD GALLERY

www.southbankcentre.co.uk

Major contemporary art exhibitions are staged in a stark 1960s setting.

➕ L6 ✉ Belvedere Road, SE1 ☎ 0844 875 0073 🕐 Mon 12–6; Tue–Wed, Sat–Sun 10–6, Thu–Fri 10–8 during exhibitions 🚇 Waterloo 🚉 Waterloo 💷 Moderate–expensive; some exhibitions free

HMS *BELFAST*

www.iwm.org.uk

Clamber up, down and around this 1938 war cruiser, visiting the

The retired 1938 war cruiser HMS Belfast

cabins, gun turrets, dining hall, bridge and boiler-room.

➕ R6 ✉ The Queen's Walk, SE1 ☎ 020 7940 6300 🕐 Mar–Oct daily 10–6; Nov–Feb 10–5 🍴 Café 🚇 London Bridge 🚊 London Bridge 💷 Expensive; children under 16 free

HOLY TRINITY, SLOANE SQUARE

www.holytrinitysloanesquare.co.uk

London's best Arts and Crafts church, designed by J.D. Sedding, has glass by Burne-Jones, William Morris and others. Note the huge east window with its 48 panels depicting saints.

➕ E9 ✉ Sloane Square, SW1 ☎ 020 7730 7270 🕐 Mon–Sat 8.30–5.30, Sun 8.30–1.30 🚇 Sloane Square 💷 Donation

HUNTERIAN MUSEUM

www.rcseng.ac.uk

See the brilliantly ghoulish exhibits, with 3,500 specimens, from the anatomical collection of John Hunter (1728–93).

➕ L4 ✉ Royal College of Surgeons, Lincoln's Inn Fields, WC2 ☎ 020 7869 6560 🕐 Tue–Sat 10–5 🚇 Holborn 💷 Free

HYDE PARK

www.royalparks.org.uk

One of London's largest open spaces, the park was tamed in the 18th century. Don't miss the views from the Serpentine Bridge, the Rose Garden or the Diana, Princess of Wales Memorial Fountain.

➕ E6 ✉ W2 ☎ 0300 061 2000 🕐 Daily 5am–midnight 🍴 Restaurant, café 🚇 Marble Arch, High Street Kensington, Hyde Park Corner 💷 Free

IMPERIAL WAR MUSEUM

www.iwm.org.uk

The museum focuses on the social impact of 20th-century warfare through film, painting and sound archives. Brand new World War I galleries were opened in 2014.

➕ M8 ✉ Lambeth Road, SE1 ☎ 020 7416 5000 🕐 Daily 10–6 🍴 Café 🚇 Lambeth North, Elephant & Castle, Waterloo 🚊 Waterloo 💷 Free

LONDON TRANSPORT MUSEUM

www.ltmuseum.co.uk

High-tech exhibits explore London's communities, and the

The Diana, Princess of Wales Memorial Fountain, Hyde Park

past and future of the capital's transport system.

🔲 K5 ⊠ Covent Garden Piazza, WC2 ☎ 020 7379 6344 🕐 Sat–Thu 10–6, Fri 11–6 🍴 Café 🚇 Covent Garden 🚉 Charing Cross 🎫 Expensive

MADAME TUSSAUD'S

www.madame-tussauds.com/London
See how many famous people you can identify, from Shakespeare to Madonna.

🔲 E3 ⊠ Marylebone Road, NW1 ☎ 0871 894 3000 🕐 Daily 9.30–5.30 🍴 Café 🚇 Baker Street 🎫 Expensive; family ticket

PETER PAN STATUE

George Frampton's statue (1912) commemorating J.M. Barrie's fictional creation, the boy who never grew up, stands in Kensingston Gardens.

🔲 B6 ⊠ Long Water, Kensington Gardens 🚇 Lancaster Gate

PETRIE MUSEUM

www.ucl.ac.uk
The ancient spoils of many Egyptologists' explorations are on display at the hard-to-find Petrie Museum (it's close to the rear of the British Museum). With 80,000 objects, it's one of the world's greatest collections of Egyptian and Sudanese archaeology.

🔲 J2 ⊠ Univeristy College London, Malet Place, WC1 ☎ 020 7679 2884 🕐 Tue–Sat 1–5 🚇 Euston Square 🎫 Free

PHOTOGRAPHERS' GALLERY

www.photonet.org.uk
An £8.7-million project has transformed an Edwardian warehouse into a state-of-the-art home for the Photographers' Gallery. The gallery has three floors of exhibition space, a bookshop and café, and hosts talks and events.

🔲 H4 ⊠ 16–18 Ramillies Street, W1 ☎ 0845 262 1618 🕐 Mon–Sat 10–6, Thu to 8, Sun 11.30–6 🚇 Oxford Circus 🎫 Free

REGENT'S PARK AND ZSL LONDON ZOO

www.royalparks.org.uk; www.zsl.org
Regent's Park has vast rose gardens, a boating lake, sports facilities and an open-air theatre in the summer. London Zoo, in its

The London Transport Museum celebrates the capital's transport system

Wax figures at Madame Tussaud's

northeastern corner, is popular with children and offers activities during holidays.

 Off map at D1–F1 ⊠ Outer Circle, Regent's Park, NW1 ☎ Park: 0300 061 2300. Zoo: 020 7722 3333 🕓 Park: daily 5am–9.30pm. Zoo: daily from 10. Closing times change seasonally 🍴 Cafés 🚇 Regent's Park, Camden Town 💷 Park: free. Zoo: expensive

ROYAL ACADEMY OF ARTS
www.royalacademy.org.uk
The Royal Academy hosts major art shows, plus the annual Summer Exhibition, held every year since 1769. Don't miss the rooftop Sackler Galleries.

⊞ H5 ⊠ Burlington House, Piccadilly, W1 ☎ 020 7300 8000 🕓 Sat–Thu 10–6, Fri 10–10 🍴 Restaurant, café 🚇 Green Park, Piccadilly 💷 Expensive

ST. BARTHOLOMEW-THE-GREAT
www.greatstbarts.com
Built in 1123, this is the City's only 12th-century monastic church, and its best surviving piece of large-scale Romanesque architecture.

⊞ N3 ⊠ West Smithfield, EC1 ☎ 020 7606 5171 🕓 Mon–Fri 8.30–5 (4pm mid-Nov to mid–Feb), Sat 8.30–4, Sun 8.30–8. Sun services at 9, 11, 6.30 🍴 Café 🚇 Barbican, Farringdon, St. Paul's 🚊 Farringdon 💷 Inexpensive

ST. JAMES'S, PICCADILLY
www.sjp.org.uk
Wren's church (1682–84), built for the local aristocracy, has a sumptuous interior. Some superb concerts are held here.

⊞ H6 ⊠ 197 Piccadilly, W1 ☎ 020 7734 4511 🕓 Daily 8–6.30 🍴 Café 🚇 Piccadilly Circus 💷 Donation

ST. KATHARINE DOCKS
www.skdocks.co.uk
Luxury yachts now fill the marina close to Tower Bridge and the Tower of London where valuable cargoes were once landed, while restaurants, bars, shops and apartments fill the former warehouses.

⊞ S6 ⊠ St. Katharine's Way, E1 ☎ 020 7488 0555 🚇 Tower Hill 🚊 Tower Gateway (DLR), Fenchurch Street 🚢 Tower Pier, St. Katharine's Pier 💷 Free

The Royal Academy of Arts

A titi monkey, one of the inhabitants of ZSL London Zoo

ST. MARGARET, LOTHBURY

www.stml.org.uk
Wren's church (1692) retains
its huge carved screen with soaring
eagle and carved pulpit tester. It
offers a weekday ministry for the
City of London.
🔲 Q4 ✉ Lothbury, EC2 ☎ 020 7726
4878 🕐 Mon–Fri 7.15–5.15 🚇 Bank
✋ Donation

SEA LIFE LONDON AQUARIUM

www.visitsealife.com/london
More than 3,000 forms of marine
life fill this aquatic spectacular.
🔲 L7 ✉ County Hall, SE1 ☎ 0871 663
1678 🕐 Daily 10–7 🚇 Westminster,
Waterloo ✋ Expensive

THE SHARD

www.theviewfromtheshard.com
Occupying floors 68–72 of
The Shard, London's newest
landmark shimmering 310m
(1,016ft) skywards, The View
offers uninterrupted 360° views
across the capital and beyond.
🔲 R6 ✉ Joiner Street, SE1
☎ 0844 499 7111 🕐 Sun–Wed 10–7;
Thu–Sat 10–10. Timed tickets, pre-booking

advised 🚇 London Bridge 🚉 London
Bridge ✋ Expensive

SOUTHWARK CATHEDRAL

http://cathedral.southwark.anglican.org
The fine stone building is power-
fully atmospheric of its medieval
origins, despite much rebuilding.
Inside, there are fine choir stalls
and some interesting monuments.
🔲 Q6 ✉ London Bridge, SE1 ☎ 020
7367 6700 🕐 Mon–Fri 8–6, Sat–Sun 8.30–
6 🍴 Café 🚇 London Bridge 🚉 London
Bridge ✋ Donation

SPENCER HOUSE

www.spencerhouse.co.uk
A lavishly restored Palladian
mansion, Spencer House is a rare
survivor of 18th-century aristocratic
St. James's and Mayfair. Eight
rooms with gilded decorations,
period paintings and furniture are
open to the public, along with the
authentically restored garden.
🔲 H6 ✉ 27 St. James's Place, SW1
☎ 020 7499 8620 🕐 Sun 10.30–4.45 (last
tour). Closed Jan and Aug. Guided tours
only 🚇 Green Park ✋ Expensive; no
children under 10

Southwark Cathedral retains a medieval appearance despite much rebuilding

Temple Church in the Inns of Court

TEMPLE CHURCH

www.templechurch.com

Begun about 1160, this private chapel built by the Knights Templar to a circular plan stands at the heart of the Inns of Court. You can visit the Temple gardens and the 16th-century Middle Temple Hall. The church hosts fine music and organ recitals; check the website for details.

🔲 M4 ✉ Temple, EC4 ☎ 020 7353 3470 🕐 Opening times vary, check website. Sun services 🚇 Temple 💷 Donation

TEMPLE OF MITHRAS

Right on the open street, the Roman temple foundations of AD240–50 testify to the cult of the Persian god Mithras.

🔲 P5 ✉ Temple Court, Queen Victoria Street, EC4 🚇 Mansion House, Bank

TRAFALGAR SQUARE

Sir Edwin Landseer's lions protect Nelson's Column, erected to commemorate the 1805 Battle of Trafalgar, at the heart of London's most iconic square. The fountains were added in 1845. Bronze statues occupy three of the plinths; the fourth hosts changing works by contemporary artists.

🔲 J6 🍴 Restaurants and cafés 🚇 Charing Cross 🚉 Charing Cross 💷 Free

VINOPOLIS

www.vinopolis.co.uk

The warren of rooms at Vinopolis is devoted to the world's wine-growing regions, with films, experts, tastings and a restaurant.

🔲 P6 ✉ 1 Bank End, SE1 ☎ 020 7940 8300 🕐 Wed 6–9.30, Thu–Fri 2–10, Sat 12–9.30, Sun 1–4; last entry 2.5 hours before closing. Prebooking essential 🚇 London Bridge 🚉 London Bridge 💷 Expensive, includes audio guide, tastings

WALLACE COLLECTION

www.wallacecollection.org

French 18th-century paintings, Old Masters, furniture, porcelain and a world-class armoury housed in a historic London town house with a good restaurant in the courtyard.

🔲 F4 ✉ Hertford House, Manchester Square, W1 ☎ 020 7563 9500 🕐 Daily 10–5 🍴 Restaurant, café 🚇 Marble Arch, Bond Street 💷 Free

Bustling Trafalgar Square, a popular meeting place

Further Afield

CANARY WHARF

www.canarywharf.com
César Pelli's soaring, pyramid-topped tower (1991) dominates a premier business district.
🔼 Off map at S5 ⊠ 1 Canada Square, Canary Wharf, E14 🕔 Public spaces are open, not buildings 🚇 Canary Wharf

CHELSEA PHYSIC GARDEN

www.chelseaphysicgarden.co.uk
This 17th-century walled garden was laid out by Sir Hans Sloane for the Society of Apothecaries.
🔼 Off map at C9 ⊠ 66 Royal Hospital Road, SW3 ☎ 020 7352 5646 🕔 Apr–Oct Tue–Fri, Sun 11–6 🍴 Café 🚇 Sloane Square 🦽 Moderate

CHISWICK HOUSE

www.chgt.org.uk
Lord Burlington's exquisite country villa (1725–29) has superb formal gardens and conservatories.
🔼 Off map at A9 ⊠ Burlington Lane, W4 ☎ 020 8995 0508 🕔 House: Apr–Oct Sun–Wed 10–5; Nov–Dec pre-booked tours only. Garden: daily 7–dusk 🍴 Café 🚇 Turnham Green 🚉 Chiswick 🦽 House: moderate. Garden: free

DULWICH PICTURE GALLERY

www.dulwichpicturegallery.org.uk
Opened in 1814, this was England's first public art gallery.
🔼 Off map at N9 ⊠ Gallery Road, SE21 ☎ 020 8693 5254 🕔 Tue–Fri 10–5, Sat–Sun 11–5 🍴 Café 🚉 North or West Dulwich 🦽 Moderate

FIREPOWER MUSEUM

www.firepower.org.uk
Exhibits here range from Roman trebuchets to an Iraqi supergun, with plenty of visitor participation.
🔼 Off map at S7 ⊠ The Royal Arsenal, Woolwich, SE18 ☎ 020 8855 7755 🕔 Tue–Sat 10–5 🍴 Café 🚉 Woolwich Arsenal ⛴ Ferry from Greenwich 🦽 Moderate

HAM HOUSE

www.nationaltrust.org.uk
The house and garden at this Thameside baroque mansion have been meticulously restored.
🔼 Off map at A10 ⊠ Ham, Richmond, Surrey, TW10 ☎ 020 8940 1950 🕔 House: Mar–Oct Sat–Thu 12–4. Gardens: Daily 11–5 🍴 Café 🚇 Richmond, then bus 371 🦽 Expensive

Historic Ham House and gardens, built in 1610 on the banks of the Thames

The Museum of London Docklands

HAMPSTEAD HEATH
www.cityoflondon.gov.uk
Hampstead Heath offers 325ha (800 acres) of open countryside to enjoy in north London.
🔶 Off map at H1 ✉ Hampstead, NW3
☎ 020 7482 7073 for visitor information
🕐 Daily 8am–dusk 🚇 Hampstead
💷 Free

JEWISH MUSEUM
www.jewishmuseum.org.uk
Exhibitions and activities on Jewish history, culture and heritage.
🔶 Off map at J1 ✉ 129–131 Albert Street, NW1 ☎ 020 7284 7384 🕐 Sat–Wed 10–5, Thu 10–9, Fri 10–2 🍴 Kosher café
🚇 Camden Town 💷 Moderate

KENWOOD HOUSE
www.english-heritage.org.uk
Restyled by Robert Adam, this country house lies outside pretty Hampstead village in north London. Its walls are hung with Rembrandts, Romneys, Vermeers and Gainsboroughs and its landscaped parkland provides grand views. In summer, evening concerts are held in the grounds.
🔶 Off map at H1 ✉ Hampstead Lane, NW3 ☎ 020 8348 1286 🕐 Daily 10–5
🍴 Café 🚇 Hampstead Heath 💷 Free

KEW GARDENS
www.kew.org
With 44,000 plants and some glorious glasshouses, the 120ha (300-acre) Royal Botanic Gardens at Kew is a magical place. Walks on tree-shaded avenues, mesmerizing flower displays, a treetop walkway for bird's-eye views and the restored Kew Palace are just some of the attractions.
🔶 Off map at A9 ✉ Queen Elizabeth's Walk, SW13 ☎ 020 8409 4400
🕐 Mar–Oct daily 9.30–6; Nov–Feb 9.30–5
🍴 Café 🚇 Hammersmith, then bus 283
🚉 Barnes, then bus 33, 72 💷 Expensive

LONDON WETLAND CENTRE
www.wwt.org.uk
The Wildfowl and Wetlands Trust administers 42ha (104 acres) of lakes, ponds, grassland and mud-flats that attract a variety of wildlife.
🔶 Off map at A9 ✉ Queen Elizabeth's Walk, SW13 ☎ 020 8409 4400 🕐 Apr–Oct daily 9.30–6; Nov–Mar 9.30–5 🍴 Café
🚇 Hammersmith, then bus 283 🚉 Barnes, then bus 33, 72 💷 Expensive

MUSEUM OF LONDON DOCKLANDS
www.museumoflondon.org.uk/docklands
The museum tells the story of London's river, port and people from Roman times until now. It also hosts events and tours.
🔶 Off map at S5 ✉ No. 1 Warehouse, West India Quay, Canary Wharf, E14 ☎ 020 7001 9844 🕐 Daily 10–6 🍴 Restaurant
🚇 West India Quay, Canary Wharf 💷 Free

V&A MUSEUM OF CHILDHOOD
www.museum of childhood.org.uk
Exhibits here explore playtime from 1600 to the present day, with Noah's arks, dolls, toy soldiers and even a model circus.
🔶 Off map at S2 ✉ Cambridge Heath Road, E2 ☎ 020 8983 5200 🕐 Daily 10–5.45 🍴 Café 🚇 Bethnal Green
🚉 Bethnal Green 💷 Free

WHITECHAPEL ART GALLERY
www.whitechapelgallery.org
The gallery is the hub of the East End contemporary art activities.
🔶 S4 ✉ 80 Whitechapel High Street, E1
☎ 020 7522 7888 🕐 Tue–Wed, Fri–Sun 11–6, Thu 11–9 🍴 Café 🚇 Aldgate East
💷 Free

HAMPTON COURT PALACE

www.hrp.org.uk

This is London's most impressive royal palace, well worth the 35-minute train journey out from central London.

When King Henry VIII dismissed Cardinal Wolsey in 1529, he took over his already ostentatious Tudor palace and enlarged it. Successive monarchs altered and repaired both the palace and its 12ha (29 acres) of Tudor and baroque gardens.

The best way to visit this huge collection of chambers, courtyards and state apartments is to follow one of the six clearly indicated routes—perhaps Henry VIII's State Apartments or the King's Apartments built for William III, immaculately restored after a devastating fire. Highlights include Henry VIII's Great Hall, which is recognized as England's finest medieval hall. William Shakespeare performed plays here between 1603 and 1604. The Chapel Royal, still in use after 450 years, should not be to be missed. Neither should the vast Tudor kitchens, built to feed Henry VIII's court, providing over 600 meals twice a day. Live cookery demonstrations are given every month; check the website for dates of these and other events.

You can easily spend a day at the palace, but allow at least three hours for your visit. Do not miss the formal Tudor gardens that reach down to the River Thames, the famous Maze and restored Privy Garden, looking now as it would have done when it was created for William III in 1702.

Children love Hampton Court, not least because there are so many events and activities designed especially for them, including costumed presentations and family audio guides and trails.

Distance: 16km (10 miles)
Journey Time: 35 min
✉ East Molesey, Surrey ☎ 0844 482 7777
🕐 Apr–Oct daily 10–6; Nov–Mar 10–4.30
🍴 Café, restaurant 🚉 Waterloo to Hampton Court 🚢 Riverboat to Hampton Court 💷 Expensive

The beautiful formal flower gardens at Hampton Court Palace

The palace's courtyard and entrance gate

WINDSOR

www.windsor.gov.uk
www.royalcollection.org.uk

Fairy-tale towers and turrets make this the ultimate royal castle. An official residence of Her Majesty the Queen, it's the oldest and largest occupied castle in the world. As it is a working royal palace, opening times can change, so it's best to phone or check the website for the latest information.

Begun by William the Conqueror and rebuilt in stone by Henry II, the castle has been embellished over the centuries. The richly decorated State Apartments are hung with paintings by Old Masters. The tombs of 10 sovereigns, including Henry VIII and Charles I, lie amid the fine Gothic architecture of St. George's Chapel, setting for the service of dedication following the marriage of Prince Charles and the Duchess of Cornwall in 2005.

Should the State Apartments or Chapel be closed, there is still much to see. The Drawings Gallery has changing exhibitions, and don't miss Queen Mary's Dolls' House, designed by Edward Lutyens. Some 1,500 craftspeople were involved in its construction.

Changing the Guard takes place at 11am daily, April to the end of July, and on alternate days for the rest of the year, weather permitting, but never on Sundays.

Outside the castle lie Windsor's pretty, medieval cobblestoned lanes, Christopher Wren's Guildhall and the delightful Theatre Royal. Beyond it, you can explore 1,950ha (4,700-acre) Windsor Great Park and cross the river footbridge to Eton, a heritage town famed for its public school.

Distance: 37km (23 miles)
Journey Time: 40–55 min
🅸 Windsor Royal Shopping, Thames Street
☎ 01753 743900 🕐 Daily Jan–Feb, Nov–Dec 9.45–4.15; Mar–Oct 9.45–5.15 (last admission 1hr 15 min before closing)
🚆 Waterloo to Windsor & Eton Riverside, Paddington to Windsor & Eton Central
Windsor Castle
☎ 01753 831118 🕐 Mar–Oct daily 9.45–5.15; Nov–Feb 9.45–4.15
💷 Expensive

Stately Windsor Castle

Great Park and the Long Walk entrance to Windsor Castle

City Tours

This section contains self-guided tours that will help you explore the sights in each of the city's regions. Each tour is designed to take a day, with a map pinpointing the recommended places along the way. There is a quick reference guide at the end of each tour, listing everything you need in that region, so you know exactly what's close by.

CITY TOURS

South Bank

With mesmerizing river views, exciting contemporary art at Tate Modern, medieval history at Southwark Cathedral, world-class concert halls and a theatrical tradition dating back to Shakespeare's time, the South Bank has plenty to entice visitors.

Morning
Start at **Tower Bridge** and set the scene for your day with high-level, panoramic views, spotting London's newest landmark, **The Shard** (▷ 75). Then stroll among the converted warehouses of Shad Thames, home to numerous shops and cafés. Join the well-signed riverside Thames Path, passing the distinctive **City Hall** (▷ 68), seat of government, and the moored war cruiser **HMS** *Belfast* (right, ▷ 70).

Mid-morning
From Tooley Street, zigzag under **London Bridge** to visit **Southwark Cathedral** (left, ▷ 74). Admire the soaring nave, choir and 16th-century Great Screen, and look for stained-glass windows depicting famous Southwark inhabitants, including Chaucer and Shakespeare. The **Harvard Chapel** reveals some of the cathedral's many links with America.

Lunch
Borough Market (right, ▷ 67) is nearby and the perfect location for lunch, especially on Thursdays to Saturdays when it is packed with enticing food stalls and the restaurants are particularly lively.

Afternoon

Return to the riverside, passing the fine 14th-century rose window in the ruins of **Winchester Palace**, to see the replica of Sir Francis Drake's galleon, *Golden Hinde II* (right, ▷ 70). Walk through medieval, cobblestoned Clink Street, once the site of a notorious prison. Passing under Southwark Bridge, restaurants, cafés and pubs with river views line the route to **Shakespeare's Globe** (▷ 46–47), a faithful reconstruction of an Elizabethan open-air theatre. The excellent guided tour of the theatre is not to be missed.

Mid-afternoon

Explore the contemporary art at **Tate Modern** (▷ 54–55) and take time for tea in its café with a view. Continue your stroll along the Thames Path, enjoying views of the architecture lining the opposite bank of the river. Have a look in the crafts studios on the lower floors of the **Oxo Tower** (left) and in nearby **Gabriel's Wharf**, before you reach **Waterloo Bridge**—you may find a second-hand books market under its arches—and the **Southbank Centre**.

Dinner

There's a vast choice of restaurants around here, but if you're up for somewhere smart with unmatched views, book a table at the **Oxo Tower Bar, Brasserie and Restaurant** (▷ 149).

Evening

With concerts by world-class musicians at the **Royal Festival Hall** (▷ 138), plays at the **National Theatre** (▷ 136) and films at **BFI Southbank** (▷ 133), you're spoiled for choice for entertainment in this part of London. Free live music events are often held in the early evening. Alternatively, a ride on the **London Eye** (▷ 28) at night is a magical experience.

Royal College
of Surgeons

Hunterian Museum

Old Curiosity Shop

Public Record Office

Dr Johnson's House

Old Bailey (Central Criminal Court)

CITY THAMESLINK STATION

London School of Economics & Political Science

Royal Courts of Justice

AA

FLEET STREET

Inns of Court

Temple Church

St Bride's Church

LUDGATE CIRCUS

Bush House (BBC)

Australia House

India House

St Clement Danes

St Mary-le-Strand Roman Bath

Temple

Middle Temple

Inner Temple

BLACKFRIARS STATION

QUEEN VICTORIA STREET

Blackfriars

Courtauld Gallery

King's College

Somerset House

Gilbert Collection

EMBANKMENT

VICTORIA

HQS Wellington (Master Mariners)

HMS President

Blackfriars Millennium Pier

Blackfriars Pier

BLACKFRIARS BRIDGE

Thames

Cleopatra's Needle

WATERLOO BRIDGES

Thames Path

Oxo Tower

Bankside Gallery

Purdy Hicks Gallery

Embankment Pier

Victoria Embankment Gardens

Savoy Pier

The London Television Centre

Festival Pier

National Theatre

BFI Southbank

STAMFORD STREET

A3200

London Nautical School

GOLDEN JUBILEE BRIDGES

Queen Elizabeth Hall

Southbank Centre

Royal Festival Hall

Hayward Gallery

Dixon House

Kings College London

Schiller University

BFI London IMAX Cinema

WATERLOO EAST STATION

Southwark

UNION STREET

Shell Centre

Concert Hall Approach

Mepham Street

THE CUT

Southwark College

Nelson Square

London Eye

Jubilee Gardens

Chicheley Street

WATERLOO STATION

YORK ROAD

Waterloo Millennium Pier

London Dungeon

County Hall

SEA LIFE London Aquarium

WESTMINSTER BRIDGE ROAD

A23

Florence Nightingale Museum

St Thomas' Hospital

Lambeth North

WESTMINSTER BRIDGE

St George's Cathedral

ST GEORGE'S CIRCUS

BOROUGH

South Bank University

LAMBETH

Archbishop's Park

Lambeth Palace

Garden Museum

A3203

Imperial War Museum

Geraldine Mary Harmsworth Park

NEWINGTON

London College of Communica...

Metropolitan Tabernacle

Elephant & Castle Leisure Centre

KENNINGTON

0   500 m

0   500 yds

L VAUXHALL   **M**   **N**

South Bank Quick Reference Guide

London Eye (▷ 28)

On a clear day you can see some 40km (25 miles) from the top of the giant wheel, right across London and as far as Windsor Castle (▷ 79). The Eye can carry 800 passengers per revolution and, with some three and a half million people stepping on board every year to enjoy the bird's-eye views, it is the most popular paid tourist attraction in Britain.

Tate Modern (▷ 54)

At the foot of the Millennium Bridge and presenting a distinctive face to the Thames, Tate Modern welcomes nearly five million visitors each year. The building itself, a converted power station, is almost as fascinating as the art within. The five-storey high Turbine Hall originally housed the electricity generators and the big spaces suit the art installations well.

ENTERTAINMENT 128

Clubs
Ministry of Sound
Film
BFI IMAX
BFI Southbank
Opera, Ballet and Concerts
Purcell Room
Queen Elizabeth Hall
Royal Festival Hall

Theatres
National Theatre
Old Vic
Shakespeare's Globe
Young Vic

EAT 140

British and Modern
Oxo Tower Bar, Brasserie
and Restaurant
European
Baltic
Cantina Vinopolis

Gastropubs/Bars
The Anchor
Anchor & Hope
Lighter Bites
Tate Modern Café

Waterloo Bridge and Thames River Walkway

Fleet Street to the Tower

On this tour, see where the Romans founded Londinium in the first century AD and discover the city's long and fascinating history through its architecture, from Sir Christopher Wren's magnificent churches to the great Tower of London, with stories to capture everyone's imagination.

Morning
Arrive early at **St. Paul's Cathedral** (right, ▷ 42–43) before the crowds descend to appreciate fully its magnificence. The cathedral opens for sightseeing at 8.30am, but there are services, usually at 7.30am and 8am, which you could attend. The branch of the pâtisserie **Paul** in St. Paul's Churchyard is the perfect place for to stop for a snack.

Mid-morning
Walk up St. Martin's Aldersgate to the **Museum of London** (left, ▷ 30–31) and spend some time exploring its excellent collection. Retracing your steps, turn left into Gresham Street. Ahead is **St. Lawrence Jewry Church**, with dark wooden pews and a gold-encrusted ceiling lit by chandeliers. Cross the Guildhall Square to visit the **Guildhall Art Gallery** (▷ 70).

Lunch
Walk down King Street and turn right into Cheapside for an early lunch at **The Café Below** (▷ 145) in the crypt of **St. Mary-le-Bow**, a Wren church with striking modern stained-glass windows. A statue of Captain John Smith (1580–1631), leader of the Virginia Colony at Jamestown, presides over the square.

CITY TOURS

After lunch, turn down Bow Churchyard passage, then turn right into Bow Lane, lined with smart shops and eateries, to cross Watling Street. On the left is the **Guild Church of St. Mary Aldermary,** last rebuilt by Wren in a Gothic style. It's worth stepping inside to admire the magnificent ceiling.

The ruins of the **Temple of Mithras** (▷ 75) stand firm amid the soaring glass-and-steel modernity of the City's financial institutions. Looking ahead you'll see the distinctive **30 St. Mary Axe** (▷ 66), known as 'The Gherkin'. Passing the great pillars of the **Mansion House**, with the Bank of England in view, do some window-shopping in the **Royal Exchange** (right, ▷ 126) before exploring the food stands in **Leadenhall Market** (▷ 125).

Afternoon
Head down Philpot Lane to the Thames, pausing to admire Wren's towering **Monument** (to the Great Fire of London) on your right. The riverside Customs House Walkway will lead you to the **Tower of London** (below, ▷ 58–59). Aim to arrive by 2pm. Ideally you will have pre-booked your entrance ticket to avoid any waiting around. First, take a tour with one of the Yeoman Warders, then spend the rest of the afternoon soaking up the history.

Evening
Sit by the Thames and enjoy the views of Tower Bridge and the south bank of the river. Walk through to **St. Katharine Docks** (▷ 73) and stroll among the smart yachts in the marina. The renovated warehouses there house a host of bars and restaurants in which to relax. Alternatively, take the Circle Line from Tower Hill to Farringdon for a gastropub experience at **The Peasant** (▷ 150).

Fleet Street to the Tower
Quick Reference Guide

Museum of London (▷ 30)

There is no better place to get an overview of the city's history, from prehistoric times to the present day, than at this museum. Its fascinating exhibits are so well displayed, it would be hard not to be engrossed. The museum even stands where the city first began, on the site of the Roman fort.

St. Paul's Cathedral (▷ 42)

Five monarchs oversaw the building of Sir Christopher Wren's masterpiece, completed in 1710, and ever since it has been the place where events of national importance are celebrated, mourned and commemorated. Come in the early evening, to listen to the choir sing evensong.

Tower of London (▷ 58)

As it is one of London's most popular sights, it's definitely worth pre-booking your entry tickets for the Tower, especially during the high-season summer months. A tour with a Yeoman Warder (known as a Beefeater) as your guide is an experience that you'll always remember.

MORE TO SEE   64

30 St. Mary Axe
All-Hallows-by-the-Tower
Bank of England Museum
Christchurch Spitalfields
Clockmakers' Museum
Dr. Johnson's House

Guildhall Art Gallery
St. Bartholomew-the-Great
St. Margaret, Lothbury
St. Katharine Docks
Temple Church
Temple of Mithras

A Routemaster bus outside St. Paul's

CITY TOURS

Covent Garden to Regent's Park

Literary associations, museums great and quirky, fine art and fun shopping all combine on this walk, which takes in busy streets and quiet corners. Here you'll find Theatreland, the heart of London's entertainment industry, lively Chinatown and Soho.

Morning

From Holborn Underground station, turn off Kingsway to enter Lincoln's Inn Fields. On its northern side, **Sir John Soane's Museum** (left, ▷ 48–49) is wonderfully atmospheric. As you cross the leafy square, look to the left to see the impressive brick buildings of Lincoln's Inn, one of the Inns of Court, and ahead to the Royal College of Surgeons, where the **Hunterian Museum** (▷ 71) is located. **The Terrace in the Fields**, in Lincoln's Inn Fields, may tempt you to a coffee before continuing on to **The Old Curiosity Shop**, built in 1567, immortalized by Charles Dickens and now displaying handmade shoes. Following St. Clement's Lane will take you through the London School of Economics' campus and out alongside the Royal Courts of Justice to the Strand, where Wren's **St. Clement Danes Church** sits on an island amid busy traffic.

Mid-morning

Continue west along the Strand to **Somerset House** (▷ 50–51) to admire the great courtyard and immerse yourself in French Impressionist art at the **Courtauld Gallery** (below, ▷ 51).

Lunch

Eat lunch in grand surroundings in Somerset House or walk up Wellington Street into lively **Covent Garden**, which is packed with cafés, restaurants and bars. **Joe Allen** (▷ 148) is a favourite. Turn left for the **Piazza** (▷ 69). Here you can shop and enjoy the buzz in the former market (right). Cross Long Acre for the trendy shops on Neal Street.

Afternoon

Passing the brightly coloured high-rise blocks on St. Giles High Street, visit **St. Giles-in-the-Fields**, a handsome church with a Palladian interior, founded by Queen Matilda in 1101 as a leper hospital. Continue down Denmark Street, famed for its music connections, and cross Charing Cross Road with Foyles, London's most famous bookshop, on the left, to reach leafy **Soho Square**. In the 17th century, this was one of the most fashionable places to live. Today the area is home to the film and recording industries and numerous pubs and restaurants.

Mid-afternoon

Leave at Frith Street, go right at the **Dog and Duck** pub and stop for refreshment as you zigzag your way through cobbled Meard Street and across Wardour Street to the lively fruit and textiles **market** on Berwick Street. A left turn on Broadwick Street and another left down Lexington Street will take you among the specialist shops of Brewer Street and back onto Wardour Street. Cross Shaftesbury Avenue and turn left into Gerrard Street, the start of **Chinatown**.

Evening

Stroll through **Chinatown** (right) and pick a restaurant that takes your fancy. Shaftesbury Avenue is the heart of **Theatreland**, **Piccadilly Circus** is a short walk away and **Soho** buzzes with restaurants and nightlife.

London Zoo

Regent's Park

St John's
Lodge

REGENT'S
PARK

Cumberland
Gate

Open Air
Theatre

Queen
Mary's
Garden

Cumberland

Market

Robert   Street

Clarence
Gardens

William Road

Regent's
College

Royal College
of Physicians

St Andrew's Place

Munster
Square

Longford   Street

Euston
Tower

EUSTON

University
College
Hospital

York Terrace West

York Terrace East

Royal Academy
of Music

MARYLEBONE

Park
Square

Regent's
Park
Crescent

Great
Portland
Street

Royal National
Orthopaedic
Hospital

Fitzroy
Square

**Madame
Tussaud's**

University
of Westminster

Central
Synagogue

BT
Tower
University
of Westminster

UCL

MARYLEBONE

MARYLEBONE HIGH STREET

PORTLAND PLACE

Langham Street

GOODGE ST

**Wallace
Collection**

Wigmore
Hall

LANGHAM
PLACE

All Saints
Church

MORTIMER   STREET

GREAT PORTLAND STREET

Eastcastle

BAKER   STREET

THAYER   STREET

WIGMORE   STREET

CAVENDISH
SQUARE

University

Margaret   Street

OXFORD

Oxford
Circus

**Photographers'
Gallery**

PORTMAN
SQUARE

ORCHARD STREET

Selfridges'

OXFORD   STREET

VERE STREET

OXFORD

NEW   BOND   STREET

REGENT

STREET

Golden
square

US
Embassy

Roosevelt
Memorial

**Handel House
Museum**

St George's
Church

New
Burlington
Place

CONDUIT

Grosvenor Hill

MAYFAIR

Burlington
Gardens

**Royal
Academy
of Arts**

St Jam
Chur

Church of the
Immaculate
Conception

PARK   LANE

A4   PICCADILLY

Green
Park

Shepherd
Market

0   500 m

0   500 yds

Spencer
House

Marlborough Hou

British Library

ST PANCRAS INTERNATIONAL STATION

THAMESLINK STATION

CROSS STATION

KING'S CROSS ROAD

Royal National Throat, Nose & Ear Hospital

ST PANCRAS

EUSTON ROAD

Eastman Dental Hospital

Mount Pleasant Postal Sorting Office

The Foundling Museum (Thomas Coram Foundation)

UPPER WOBURN PLACE

British Medical Association

Coram's Fields

Charles Dickens Museum

Petrie Museum

GOWER STREET

University of London

Brunswick Shopping Centre

National Hospital for Sick Children (Great Ormond St)

Gray's Inn

RADA

National Hospital for Neurology & Neurosurgery

BLOOMSBURY

Russell Square

Inns of Court & School of Law

University College London

Royal London Homeopathic Hospital

Gray's Inn Square

THEOBALD'S ROAD

British Museum

MONTAGUE PLACE

RUSSELL SQUARE

HOLBORN

The Cartoon Museum

BLOOMSBURY WAY

HIGH HOLBORN

HOLBORN

YMCA

NEW OXFORD STREET

Holborn

Sir John Soane's Museum

Lincoln's Inn

ST GILES CIRCUS

Point

New Oxford Street

Royal College of Surgeons

Hunterian Museum

Tottenham Court Road

ST GILES

Oasis Sports Centre

Old Curiosity Shop

London School of Economics & Political Science

Royal Courts of Justice

SOHO

CAMBRIDGE CIRCUS

ENDELL STREET

Wild Street

ALDWYCH

Bush House (BBC)

Australia House

St Clement Danes

CHINATOWN

SHAFTESBURY AVENUE

Royal Opera House

Covent Garden Piazza

India House

STRAND

St Mary-le-Strand

Courtauld Gallery

Roman Bath

London Trocadero

Leicester Square

St Paul's Church

London Transport Museum

King's College

Temple

Somerset House

Eros

Piccadilly Circus

National Portrait Gallery

National Gallery

St Martin-in-the-Fields

Benjamin Franklin House

Trafalgar Square

Nelson's Column

CHARING CROSS STATION

Royal Society of Arts

Cleopatra's Needle

WATERLOO BRIDGE

Savoy Pier

WATERLOO BRIDGES

Festival Pier

Queen Elizabeth Hall

BFI Southbank

Admiralty Arch

THE MALL

WHITEHALL

Hispaniola

GOLDEN JUBILEE BRIDGES

Hayward Gallery

Royal Festival Hall

Duke of York Column

Old Admiralty

Old War Office

DEFRA

J

K

L

Covent Garden to Regent's Park
Quick Reference Guide

British Museum (▷ 16)

This is one of the world's greatest museums, where you can travel the globe through exhibits from every civilization. With eight million artefacts in the collection, you may find you visit more than once.

Sir John Soane's Museum (▷ 48)

Of all London's quirky small museums this one tops the bill, with architect Sir John Soane's eclectic collection packing every surface of his former home.

Somerset House (▷ 50)

In summer, fountains play in the courtyard; in winter it becomes an outdoor ice rink. Whenever you visit, there's likely to be something happening, and the art collection at the Courtauld Gallery is superb.

MORE TO SEE	64

British Library
Charles Dickens Museum
Cleopatra's Needle
Covent Garden Piazza
Eros
Foundling Museum
Handel House Museum

Hunterian Museum
London Transport Museum
Madame Tussaud's
Petrie Museum
Photographers' Gallery
Regent's Park and ZSL London Zoo
Wallace Collection

Westminster and St. James's

Westminster Abbey, the Houses of Parliament, Buckingham Palace, Trafalgar Square—some of London's most famous landmarks are located in Westminster. Follow in the footsteps of royalty as you take in famous art galleries, London's prettiest royal park and some upscale shopping.

Morning
Begin your day at **Trafalgar Square** (▷ 75), where Sir Edwin Landseer's lions proudly protect Nelson's Column. Presiding over its northern side, the **National Gallery** (▷ 32–33) shows Western European art in a stately setting. Next door, the **National Portrait Gallery** (above, ▷ 34–35) puts faces to famous names down the centuries. Both galleries have good cafés, but you may also like the nearby **Café in the Crypt** at **St. Martin-in-the-Fields** (▷ 138). Perhaps book for a candlelit concert while you are there.

Mid-morning
Walk down Whitehall to visit the **Banqueting House** (right, ▷ 14–15), noted for its Rubens ceiling, and to see the colourful **Horse Guards** and **Cenotaph** war memorial. You soon arrive at **Big Ben** and the **Houses of Parliament** (▷ 22–23). There are splendid views of the River Thames from Westminster Bridge, immortalized by poet William Wordsworth and Impressionist Claude Monet. **Westminster Abbey** (▷ 62–63) lies across the square.

Lunch
Turn up Storey's Gate to **St. James's Park** (▷ 40–41), perhaps picking up a sandwich en route to eat in this pretty royal park. Alternatively, try **Inn the Park** (▷ 148). You will pass the **Churchill War Rooms** (▷ 68) beneath a sweeping flight of steps, watched over by the statue of an imperious Clive of India, and may wish to return there after lunch. Stroll among the park's trees and flowerbeds and watch the ducks, geese and pelicans feeding on the lake.

Afternoon

Crossing the Mall, a wide ceremonial route packed with crowds on great occasions, you will see **Buckingham Palace** (above, ▷ 18–19) on your left, fronted by the Queen Victoria Memorial. Walk up the Mall to get a closer look at the palace, or cross to Marlborough Road alongside the red-brick **St. James's Palace.** A working royal palace, setting for official receptions, it houses the Household Office of Prince William and Prince Harry. **Clarence House** (▷ 68), home of Prince Charles and the Duchess of Cornwall, is on the far side of the palace.

Mid-afternoon

St. James's Street is lined with old-established businesses such as wine merchant **Berry Bros & Rudd** (▷ 123). Turn right into Jermyn Street for more quintessentially British shops, many carrying the Royal Warrant. Walking through the elegant Piccadilly Arcade brings you into Piccadilly, where **Fortnum & Mason** (▷ 124) is the perfect place for afternoon tea. **Hatchards** (▷ 125), booksellers since 1797, is next door. Visit **St. James's, Piccadilly** (▷ 73), Wren's church for the local aristocracy. There may be a concert on there in the evening.

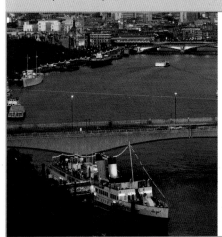

Evening

If you like the Grand Café tradition, **The Wolseley** (▷ 151) is for you. Or dress up for a meal at **Greenhouse** (▷ 147) in Mayfair. Alternatively, reserve an evening Thames River **dinner cruise** (left, ▷ 56–57).

MAYFAIR

5 Church of the Immaculate Conception

Royal Academy of Arts

St James's Church

Berkeley

Square

South Street

Farm Street

Hay's Mews

Chesterfield Hill

Charles Street

Waverton Street

Hay Hill

Berkeley Street

Dover Street

Albemarle Street

Old Bond Street

Burlington Gardens

Vigo Street

Swallow Street

Sackville Street

Vine Street

PICCADILLY

Duke Street

Jermyn Street

Bury Street

St James's Street

Ryder Street

King Street

6 Curzon Street

Derby Street

Market Mews

Shepherd Market

Shepherd Street

Hertford Street

Down Street

Brick Street

Old Park Lane

A4

Clarges Mews

Clarges Street

Bolton Street

Half Moon Street

Mayfair Place

Stratton Street

Curzon St

Green Park

PICCADILLY

A4 ST JAMES'S STREET

Park Place

St James's Place

Little St James's Street

Arlington Street

Spencer House

Marlborough House

Queen Alexandra Memorial

Cleveland Row

St James's Palace

Stable Yard Rd

Queen's Chapel

Clarence House

Lancaster House

The Mall

Apsley House

Wellington Arch

HYDE PARK CORNER

PARK LANE

Hamilton Place

Green Park

Constitution Hill

Buckingham Palace

Queen Victoria Memorial

St James's

Spur Road

Birdcage Walk

7 DUKE OF WELLINGTON PLACE

A302

GROSVENOR PLACE

Halkin Street

Headfort Place

Montrose Place

Chapel Street

Upper Belgrave Street

Buckingham Palace Gardens

Queen's Gallery

Royal Mews

BUCKINGHAM GATE

Wellington Barracks

Catherine Place

Wilfred Street

Castle Lane

Palace Street

BUCKINGHAM GATE

Petty

Westminster City School

Westminster City Hall

Spenser Street

8 Eccleston Mews

Chester Street

Little Chester Street

Wilton Street

Wilton Crescent Mews

BELGRAVE PLACE

HOBART PLACE

BEESTON PLACE

GROSVENOR GARDENS

LOWER GROSVENOR PLACE

Eaton Lane

Warwick Row

BRESSENDEN PLACE

Cardinal Place Shopping Centre

Palace Street

Allington Street

VICTORIA STREET

A302 VICTORIA STREET

Howick Place

EATON SQUARE

Eccleston Street

Chester Row

Lower Belgrave Street

Eaton Mews South

Chester Square

Ebury Street

GROSVENOR GARDENS ROAD

PALACE STREET

Terminus Place

VICTORIA BUS STATION

VICTORIA STATION

A3214

Eaton Place

WILTON RD

A202

Westminster Cathedral

Carlisle Place

Ambrosden Avenue

Morpeth Terrace

Francis Street

Thirleby Road

KING'S SCHOLARS' PASSAGE

KING'S ROAD

ECCLESTON STREET

Eaton West

Eaton Mews

Elizabeth St

Ebury Mews

Ebury Street

Gerald Road

Chester Square

Victoria Place Shopping Centre

The Colonnades Shopping Centre

Gillingham Street

BRIDGE PL

Queen Mother Sports Centre

Stillington Street

Willow Place

Vauxhall Bridge Road

VAUXHALL BRIDGE

ROCHESTER

9 VICTORIA COACH STATION

Semley Place

Elizabeth Bridge

BUCKINGHAM PALACE ROAD

A3214

Hugh Street

Eccleston Square

Belgrave Road

Eccleston Mews

BELGRAVE ROAD

Denbigh Street

Churton St

Tachbrook St

Ebury Bridge

Cundy Street

WARWICK

0   500 m
0   500 yds

F   G   H

Leicester Square

National Portrait Gallery

National Gallery

Trafalgar Square

Nelson's Column

Benjamin Franklin House

KING CHARLES I ISLAND

St Martin-in-the-Fields

Proud Gallery

Charles I Statue

Royal Society of Arts

Cleopatra's Needle

CHARING CROSS STATION

Embankment

Admiralty Arch

Carlton House

Duke of York Column

Institute of Contemporary Arts (ICA)

Old Admiralty

DEFRA

Hispaniola

ST JAMES'S

St James's Park

Horse Guards Parade

Privy Council Office

Old War Office

Banqueting House

Ministry of Defence

Thames River Cruise

Waterloo Millennium Pier

Churchill War Rooms

Foreign & Commonwealth Office

Cenotaph

Government Offices

Derby Gate

Portcullis House

Westminster Millennium Pier

Guards Museum

Birdcage Walk

Old Queen Street

Queen Elizabeth II Conference Centre

Middlesex Guildhall

PARLIAMENT SQUARE

PARLIAMENT BRIDGE STREET

Big Ben

WESTMINSTER BRIDGE

 nistry of Justice

Central Hall

St Margaret's Westminster

Oliver Cromwell Statue

Palace of Westminster

Broadway Shopping Centre

New Scotland Yard

Department of Trade & Industry

Westminster Abbey

Church House

Westminster School

Jewel Tower

Houses of Parliament

Burghers of Calais

Victoria Tower Gardens

Home Office

St John's Concert Hall

WESTMINSTER

St John's Garden

Thames House

LAMBETH BRIDGE

The Greycoat Hospital

Gordon Hospital

Millbank Tower

Millbank Millennium Pier

Tate Britain

CITY TOURS

103

Westminster and St. James's
Quick Reference Guide

TOP 25 **SIGHTS AND EXPERIENCES**

Banqueting House (▷ 14)
Inigo Jones's 17th-century architectural masterpiece has a magnificent Rubens ceiling.

Buckingham Palace (▷ 18)
The summer opening of this royal residence and office of the Royal Household is not to be missed.

Houses of Parliament (▷ 22)
Britain is governed from this landmark Victorian Gothic building on the banks of the Thames.

National Gallery (▷ 32)
The superb collection gives a overview of European painting from Giotto to Cézanne.

National Portrait Gallery (▷ 34)
The famous and the infamous, past and present, are portrayed in paintings and photographs.

St. James's Park (▷ 40)
Tree-filled, surrounded by palaces and with a lake at its heart, this is the prettiest of the royal parks.

Tate Britain (▷ 52)
Tate Britain exhibits British art from 1500 to the 21st century, with a whole gallery devoted to Turner.

Thames River Cruise (▷ 56)
Sit down, relax and enjoy views of some of the most beautiful and interesting buildings in London.

Westminster Abbey (▷ 62)
The vast abbey is full of exquisite detail and monuments. Herein lies a pageant of British history.

MORE TO SEE	64

Apsley House
Benjamin Franklin House
Churchill War Rooms
Clarence House
Green Park

Royal Academy of Arts
St. James's, Piccadilly
Spencer House
Trafalgar Square

SHOP	118

Art and Antiques
Agnews
Books
Hatchards
Department Stores
Fortnum & Mason

Fashion
Turnbull & Asser
Food and Drink
Berry Bros & Rudd

ENTERTAINMENT	128

Bars
Trader Vic's
Clubs
Dover Street
Comedy
The Comedy Store
Dancing
The Ritz

Film
Institute of Contemporary Arts
(ICA)
Opera, Ballet and Concerts
St James's, Piccadilly
St Martin-in-the-Fields

EAT	140

Asian
Tamarind
British and Modern
Portrait Restaurant
The Wolseley
Famous Chefs
Le Gavroche
Greenhouse

International
Gaucho
Lighter Bites
Inn the Park

Around Hyde Park

A feast of world-class museums and music put South Kensington firmly on every visitor's must-see list. Adjoining Hyde Park, Kensington Gardens come complete with a romantic royal palace and memories of Diana, Princess of Wales, who lived there.

CITY TOURS

Morning
At **South Kensington Underground** station there's a passage marked 'To the Museums'. Follow it, or come up to street level for a fortifying breakfast at one of the many cafés and pâtisseries that crowd this popular area. You are heading for the Cromwell Road and three world-class museums: the **Victoria and Albert Museum** (left, ▷ 60–61), the **Natural History Museum** (▷ 36–37) and the **Science Museum** (▷ 44–45). They are free, so you could pop into each one to get an idea of their riches, or spend the morning engrossed in the subjects that interest you most.

Mid-morning
All three museums have **cafés** to retreat to for sustenance. The café at the V&A is located in what was the world's first museum restaurant, in rooms intended as a showpiece of modern design and craftsmanship. During summer you can eat outdoors. The cafés at the Science and Natural History museums are particularly child-friendly.

Lunch
Walk up Exhibition Road towards **Hyde Park** (▷ 71), turning left at Prince Consort Road to view the stately red-brick **Royal College of Music** and to approach the elliptical **Royal Albert Hall** (▷ 137). The **Café Consort** upstairs is a good lunch spot and you could perhaps make reservations for a concert or tour. Look at the detail on the frieze that rings this distinctive domed building and, going west, don't miss the reliefs and *sgraffito* that decorate the facade of the building opposite, previously occupied by the Royal College of Organists.

Afternoon

Cross Kensington Gore to the **Albert Memorial** (right, ▷ 66), an ornate fantasy in glittering gold by George Gilbert Scott. Stroll through **Kensington Gardens** (▷ 24–25) to the Diana, Princess of Wales Memorial Fountain in adjacent Hyde Park. Then take the path back through Kensington Gardens via the Round Pond to **Kensington Palace** (▷ 24–25).

Mid-afternoon

Tour Kensington Palace and take afternoon tea in **The Orangery** (▷ 149). Leaving by the Kensington Palace Gardens exit and 'billionaires' row' of embassies, cross Kensington Church Street to the specialist shops and galleries along **Holland Street**. Turn left down **Kensington Church Walk** for exquisite little shops, courtyard houses and gardens. This is secret, village-like London yet only seconds away from busy Kensington High Street.

Dinner

Babylon (▷ 144), with its rooftop gardens and fabulous views across London, is nearby, as is Kensington favourite **Maggie Jones's** (▷ 148). Or you could take the bus to Knightsbridge, go shopping and relax in the **Champagne Bar** at **Harrods** (below, ▷ 125).

5

Moscow Road
Bayswater
Popular Place
Caroline Place
Queens
Ice Rink &
Bowl
Orme
Court
Queensway

QUEENSWAY
INVERNESS
PLACE
B411
Queensborough Terrace
LEINSTER TERRACE
Craven Hill
Craven Hill
Mews

Porchester Gardens
Craven Hill Gardens
Leinster Mews
Lancaster

CRAVEN HILL

WESTBOURNE
STREET

LANCASTER TERRACE
Elms
Mews
Lancaster
Gate
Lancaster
Gate
Westbourne
Gate

Marlborough
Gate

A402
BAYSWATER

Black Lion
Gate
Inverness
Terrace Gate

Portchester
Gate
Lancaster
Gate

ROAD

Speke's
Monument

*Kensington
Gardens*

Peter Pan
Statue

Physical Energy
Statue

6

Jubilee
Walk

The Broad Walk

*Round
Pond*

Serpentine
Gallery

Kensington
Palace

Palace Gardens

Palace
Avenue

The Broad Walk

West Carriage

7
KENSINGTON
CHURCH
STREET

KENSINGTON ROAD

Palace
Gate

**Albert
Memorial**

Alexandra
Gate

Kensington
Market
Court

Kensington Court

HYDE PARK GATE

Young
Street

Kensington
Square

Kensington Court
Ansdell St
Thackeray St

Cambridge
Place

Albert
Place

Kensington

Douro Place

De Vere Gardens

PALACE GATE

Hyde Park Gate

Palace
Gate Court

Prince's Gate

Queen's
Gate

KENSINGTON GORE

Royal College
of Art

Jay Mews

Royal
**Albert
Hall**

Royal
Geographical
Society

Albert Court

Exhibition

Imperial College
of Science

Prince Consort Road

Royal College
of Music

Exhibition Road

Kensington
Gate

KENSINGTON

St Alban's Grove

Victoria Grove

Canning Pl

Launceston Place

Queen's Gate

Queen's Gate

Queen's Gate Mews

Queen's Gate Terrace

Petersham Place

Petersham
Mews

Elvaston
Place

Elvaston
Mews

Ayrton Road

Imperial
College

Imperial College

Imperial College Road

Frankland
Road

**Science
Museum**

8
Cottesmore
Gardens

Eldon Road

Stanford Rd

Kynance
Mews

Victoria Rd

Cornwall
Gardens

Cornwall
Gardens

Grenville Place

Petersham
Place

Queen's Gate Place

Queen's Gate Place Mews

Queen's Gate
Gardens

Wells Way

Callendar Road

**Natural History
Museum**

Earth
Galleries

Lexham
Gardens

Cromwell
Hospital

Emperor's Gate
McLeod's Mews

Southwell
Gardens

B325

Gardens

Superstore

A4 CROMWELL ROAD

Gloucester
Road

Ashburn Pl

Ashburn

GLOUCESTER ROAD

CROMWELL

ROAD

Queensberry
Place

Stanhope
Mews East
Stanhope

Queen's

Harrington Road

Reece Mews

Bute St

ROAD A3218

9
Courtfield
Gardens

Collingham
Gardens

Courtfield
Gardens

Colbeck
Mews

Courtfield
Road

Ashburn
Gardens
Gloucester
Road

Stanhope Gardens

West Cromwell

Cranley
Place

BROMPTON

Hesper Mews

**SOUTH
KENSINGTON**

Wetherby Gardens

Bina Gardens

Rosary Gardens

Cranley
Gardens

Onslow
Square

A

B

OLD

0   500 m
0   500 yds

25 SIGHTS AND EXPERIENCES

Kensington Palace and Gardens (▷ 24)

This historic royal palace, set in the 110ha (275-acre) Kensington Gardens, was home to Queen Victoria and more recently Diana, Princess of Wales.

Knightsbridge Shopping (▷ 26)

Knightsbridge's shops enthral the most dedicated fashionista, with window displays to delight the eye. Don't miss those famous London landmarks Harvey Nichols and Harrods.

Natural History Museum (▷ 36)

With everything that you have ever wanted to know about the natural world and a whole lot more under one roof, the museum is a truly fascinating place.

Science Museum (▷ 44)

With exhibits ranging from Stephenson's steam locomotive *Rocket* to a space capsule, and with an IMAX cinema and plenty of hand's-on fun, the museum makes science entertaining.

Victoria and Albert Museum (▷ 60)

This wonderful treasure house of decorative arts, one of the largest collections of its kind in the world, delights, inspires and often surprises.

CITY TOURS

Further Afield

Birthplace of Henry VIII and Elizabeth I, home to the National Maritime Museum and famed for the Royal Observatory, Greenwich (▷ 20–21) makes a great escape from central London, with open parkland, river views and a lively market selling food and crafts.

CITY TOURS

Morning
The perfect way to travel to Greenwich is by boat, as the royals did in centuries past, for the **Old Royal Naval College** (above, ▷ 20) presents a splendid baroque facade to the river. Alternatively, the Docklands Light Railway (DLR) gets you there quickly. Make your first stop the **Discover Greenwich** tourist information centre, which has an excellent exhibition on the **Maritime Greenwich World Heritage Site** and the very good **Old Brewery** café/bar (tel 0203 327 1280). Located in the Pepys Building, it is close to the magnificent *Cutty Sark*, the world's last tea clipper, restored after serious fire damage.

Mid-morning
Cross Romney Road to visit the **National Maritime Museum** (right, ▷ 21) and delve into all matters nautical, with plenty of hands-on exhibits. A colonnade links the museum with the elegant Palladian-style **Queen's House**, designed by Inigo Jones in the 17th-century. Today it houses a fine art collection with works by Gainsborough, Reynolds and Turner. Back across Romney Road, visit the neo-classical **Chapel of St. Peter and St. Paul** and the magnificent **Painted Hall** of the Old Royal Naval College. The ceiling here took 19 years to complete and the artist, James Thornhill, was eventually knighted for his labours. It was here that the body of Admiral Lord Nelson lay in state after the Battle of Trafalgar.

Lunch
There's a good **restaurant** downstairs in the Old Royal Naval College, or for something less formal you could choose to return to the **Old Brewery** in the Pepys Building.

Afternoon
Now head up the hill in Greenwich Park to the **Royal Observatory** (above, ▷ 21), commissioned by Charles II and designed by Wren in 1675 with the purpose of finding longitude at sea. The Time Galleries' exhibits, interactive **Astronomy Centre** and the **Peter Harrison Planetarium** are fascinating. Here you can stand astride the **Greenwich Meridian** line.

Mid-afternoon
Covering 74ha (183 acres) **Greenwich Park** is the oldest enclosed royal park, with rose gardens, a flower garden, lake, wilderness deer park and fine views across the Thames to Docklands and the City of London (left). Follow a path leading to Regency houses on Crooms Hill and continue downhill to the lively weekend **market**, packed with food stalls, crafts and small design shops.

Dinner
Take the DLR to **Canary Wharf** (▷ 76), in the heart of Docklands, to eat at the 18th-century waterside pub **The Gun** (▷ 147), once the haunt of smugglers and Lord Nelson's favourite trysting place.

CITY TOURS

Stanmore
Edgware
Finchley
Hendon

Kenwood House
Hampstead Heath
Golders Hill Park

Jewish Museum
Primrose Hill

Wembley
Willesden
Kilburn
Paddington

Wormwood Scrubs

EALING

Portobello Road Market
Kensington Gardens
Hyde Park
Green Park
Holland Park

HAMMERSMITH
WESTMINSTER

Windsor
Chiswick House
Chelsea Physic Garden
Battersea Park

Syon Park
Kew Gardens
London Wetland Centre
Thames

RICHMOND
Richmond Park
Putney
WANDSWORTH
Wandsworth Common
Clapham
Clapham Common

Tooting Bec Common

Ham House
Ham Common
Wimbledon Common
Streatham

KINGSTON UPON THAMES
Wimbledon
MERTON

Bushy Park
Morden Hall Park
Mitcham

Hampton Court Palace
Hampton Court Park
Morden
Morden Park
Mitcham Common

Poulter Park

SUTTON

Fryent Country Park

Alexandra Park

114

Wood Green
A10
A1055
Tottenham
HARINGEY
A105
A503
Finsbury Park
A1
Dalston
HACKNEY
Shoreditch
A10
A107
ONDON
CITY
lames's rk
SOUTHWARK
A100
Burgess Park
ixton
ockwell Park
A23
A212
A314
A212
A215
A33
A236
A222
CROYDON
A212
A33

Epping Forest
A406
M11
A113
WALTHAM FOREST
4
REDBRIDGE
A1400
Walthamstow
A12
Walthamstow Marshes
A104
Wanstead Park
Leytonstone
A406
Leyton
Wanstead Flats
A117
Hackney Marshes
A12
A118
Stratford
East Ham
Victoria Park
A117
V&A Museum of Childhood
Mile End Park
A11
NEWHAM
A124
A13
A1020
Whitechapel Art Gallery
A12
A13
Museum of London Docklands
Canary Wharf
Southwark Park
Thames
Firepower Museum
Woolwich
GREENWICH
Greenwich Park
Woolwich Common
A207
New Cross
A2
Black Heath
A205
Eltham Common
Oxleas Wood
Peckham
Peckham Rye Park
A20
A2
Dulwich Picture Gallery
LEWISHAM
A20
Dulwich Park
A212
Dulwich
A20
A205
Elmstead Wood
A208
Crystal Palace
Crystal Palace Park
Beckenham Place Park
A21
Sundridge Park
A232
A222
Petts Wood
A232
Jubilee Country Park
BROMLEY
A232
A232
A2022
A212

0   4 km
0   2 miles

Further Afield Quick Reference Guide

 SIGHTS AND EXPERIENCES

Greenwich (▷ 20)
The ideal way to spend a Sunday is to take a cruise on the Thames to Greenwich, a UNESCO World Heritage Site. Visit the great maritime sights and the Royal Observatory, take a leisurely stroll in historic Greenwich Park and shop in the lively crafts market.

Portobello Road Market (▷ 38)
Dedicate a Saturday to exploring the shops and stalls of an antiques market like no other. Whatever you're looking for, be it glass, china, curios or jewellery, it's likely you'll find it here and searching for treasure and bargaining with the dealers is all part of the fun.

Kew Gardens (▷ 77)
Flowers, trees, plants and shrubs from around the globe grow in swathes across landscapes and fill giant glasshouses in the world's most famous botanical garden. Take the treetop walkway for a bird's eye view.

MORE TO SEE	64

Canary Wharf
Chelsea Physic Garden
Chiswick House
Dulwich Picture Gallery
Firepower Museum
Ham House
Hampstead Heath

Jewish Museum
Kenwood House
London Wetland Centre
Museum of London Docklands
V&A Museum of Childhood
Whitechapel Art Gallery

Shop

Whether you're looking for the best local products, a department store or a quirky boutique, you'll find them all in London. In this section shops are listed alphabetically.

SHOP

Introduction

If England really is a nation of shop-keepers, then London is the head office. You can find almost anything if you are determined enough. London has long been the world's marketplace and you'll find saris and spices as easily as rare reggae records, depending on the district—it really pays to explore beyond the West End. For shoppers, the choice ranges from vibrant street markets to legendary department stores and from offbeat boutiques to smart galleries of paintings and antiques.

Contemporary and Traditional

It is the range that excites visitors, whether in cutting-edge contemporary, classics or antiques. London has outrageous fashion, bolstered by the annual crop of imaginative art-, fashion- and design-school graduates. By contrast, long-established shopping streets, such as Oxford Street and Kensington High Street, offer mass-market goods, while markets such as Camden Lock and Portobello Road are eclectic, ethnic and inexpensive.

Buying a London Memory

London's souvenirs range from tatty to tasteful. Ever since the Swinging Sixties, anything with a

---

BEST OF BRITISH

Take home some British souvenirs with a difference. You can buy beautifully crafted umbrellas and walking sticks from James Smith & Sons (✉ 53 New Oxford Street, WC1). For a good British cheese buy a Stilton, all ready and packed, from Paxton & Whitfield (✉ 93 Jermyn Street, SW1). If you want to try some British recipes go to Books for Cooks (✉ 4 Blenheim Crescent, W11) for a large selection of cookbooks. Tea addicts should head to The Tea House (✉ 15A Neal Street, WC2) for a choice of blends and some stylish teapots. English herbs, oils and toiletries from Culpeper Herbalists (✉ 8 The Market, Covent Garden, WC2) make great presents.

Clockwise from top: The elegant arcades of Leadenhall Market; handmade shoes for sale in St. James's; one of the antiques shops in Camden Passage; the central well

Union Jack flag on it has sold well. For high quality, go to the museum shops. Gifts at the shop in Buckingham Palace Mews include the Queen Victoria range of china, a mini-throne for a charm bracelet or a guardsman puppet. The Victoria and Albert Museum, British Museum and National Gallery also stock quality items inspired by their diverse collections—budget permitting, you can do a full-scale family gift shop at any of these. Tate Modern has fine handcrafted jewellery, while the Museum of London is particularly good for souvenirs and books about London. At the National Portrait Gallery, you will find books on historical figures and British history, as well as a good supply of postcards and posters.

The Ultimate British Buy

Go to St. James's or Knightsbridge to purchase traditional British-made goods such as tweed jackets, handmade shoes or delicate fragrances, elegant china, floral printed fabrics and cashmere sweaters. Visit Burlington Arcade (▷ panel below) for its specialist upscale shops in a historic setting. Burberry and Aquascutum are synonymous with raincoats. Harrods has been trading for some 150 years; Selfridges was the country's first department store; and Liberty fabrics are still exotic and luxurious. Their January and July sales are major events on any serious shopper's calendar.

SHOP THE SHOP

Charles Dickens would recognize many London shops. Burlington Arcade, off Piccadilly, is an 18th-century covered shopping mall, with a liveried beadle to maintain decorum. Many shops display the royal insignia, showing that they supply members of the Royal Household with everything from brushes to jewels (www.royalwarrant. org). For instance, John Lobb (✉ 88 Jermyn Street, SW1) custom-makes shoes and boots for the royal family—and for you, at a price.

in Liberty; Lobb on St. James's Street, selling exclusive made-to-measure shoes; Fortnum & Mason in Piccadilly, renowned for its luxury foods and top-notch wines

SHOP

Directory

Fleet Street to the Tower

Street Markets
Leadenhall Market
Petticoat Lane
Spitalfields Market

Covent Garden to Regent's Park

Art and Antiques
Grays Antique Market
Books
Forbidden Planet
Stanfords
Department Stores
Liberty
Selfridges
Fashion
Browns
Food and Drink
Villandry
Health and Beauty
Neal's Yard Remedies
Homeware
Aram Designs Ltd
Benjamin Pollock's Toyshop
Heal's
Thomas Goode Ltd
Toys
Hamleys

Westminster and St. James's

Art and Antiques
Agnews
Books
Hatchards
Department Stores
Fortnum & Mason
Fashion
Turnbull & Asser
Food and Drink
Berry Bros & Rudd

Around Hyde Park

Department Stores
Harrods
Harvey Nichols
Peter Jones
Fashion
Jimmy Choo
Lulu Guinness
Urban Outfitters

Further Afield

Books
Books for Cooks
Fashion
Brora
Food and Drink
Rococo
Homeware
Ceramica Blue
Contemporary Applied Arts
Designers Guild
Shopping Centres
Westfield London
Street Markets
Bermondsey Market
Camden Markets

SHOP

Shopping A–Z

AGNEWS

www.agnewsgallery.com

This internationally renowned art gallery, in business since 1817, specializes in European Old Masters and British art from the 17th to the 20th centuries.

➕ G6 ✉ 35 Albermarle Street, W1
☎ 020 7290 9250 🕐 By appointment
🚇 Green Park

ARAM DESIGNS LTD

www.aram.co.uk

Aram's international modern designs are displayed on five floors. Stock includes furniture, lighting and glass.

➕ K4 ✉ 110 Drury Lane, WC2 ☎ 020 7557 7557 🕐 Mon–Sat 10–6 🚇 Covent Garden

BENJAMIN POLLOCK'S TOYSHOP

www.pollocks-coventgarden.co.uk

Selling traditional toy theatres and collectable toys for adults and children, this toy shop is delightfully different.

➕ K5 ✉ 44 The Market, WC2 ☎ 020 7379 7866 🕐 Mon–Sat 10.30–6, Sun 11–4 🚇 Covent Garden

BERMONDSEY MARKET

Rise before dawn on a Friday and join the bargain-hunters. The market is best for small items.

PRIVATE GALLERIES

An indispensable tool to help you find out about commercial art galleries in London is the monthly *Galleries* magazine (www.galleries.co.uk), which is available free from most galleries. With its maps and specialist subject index, information can be called up by area as well as subject.

➕ R8 ✉ Bermondsey Square, SE1
☎ 020 7240 7405 🕐 Fri 5am–3pm
🚇 London Bridge

BERRY BROS & RUDD

www.bbr.com

Wine merchant Berry Bros & Rudd has traded in the same shop since 1698. Prices range from around £5 to £5,000. The own-label bottles are good value.

➕ H6 ✉ 3 St. James's Street, SW1
☎ 0800 280 2440 🕐 Mon–Fri 10–6, Sat 10–5 🚇 Green Park

BOOKS FOR COOKS

www.booksforcooks.com

Browse the amazing selection of books about cooking and cuisine. Then head to the café, where recipes are tested, for some refreshments. Cookery classes are held in the demonstration kitchen.

➕ Off map ✉ 4 Blenheim Crescent, W11
☎ 020 7221 1992 🕐 Tue–Sat 10–6.
Closed last 3 weeks in Aug and 10 days over Christmas and New Year 🚇 Ladbroke Grove

BRORA

www.brora.co.uk

Choose from cashmere in an array of shades for men, women and children. It is pricey, but the quality is superb.

➕ Off map ✉ 344 King's Road, SW3
☎ 020 7352 3697 🕐 Mon–Sat 10–6, Sun 12–5 🚇 Sloane Square

BROWNS

www.brownsfashion.com

This boutique has long led the fashion pack, offering chic designs at grown-up prices.

➕ F4 ✉ 23–27 South Molton Street, W1
☎ 020 7514 0016 🕐 Mon–Sat 10–6.30
🚇 Bond Street

SHOP

Bookshop cafés to seek out include the cake shop connected by a passage in the History section of London Review Bookshop (✉ 14 Bury Place, WC1 ☎ 020 7269 9030) and the café next to the Jazz department of Foyles (✉ 113–19 Charing Cross Road, WC2 ☎ 020 7440 3207). Waterstone's superstore on Piccadilly has a café, a bar and a restaurant with great views.

CAMDEN MARKETS

www.camdenlock.net
The small, vibrant market at Camden is famous for alternative and vintage fashion.
✚ Off map ✉ Camden High Street to Chalk Farm Road, NW1 ⊙ Daily 9.30–6 with more stalls at weekends ⊛ Camden Town, Chalk Farm

CERAMICA BLUE

www.ceramicablue.co.uk
A feast of colour for the table and kitchen, handpicked from designers worldwide, Ceramica Blue is good for unusual gifts.
✚ Off map ✉ 10 Blenheim Crescent, W11 ☎ 020 7727 0288 ⊙ Daily Mon–Sat 10–6, Sun 12–5 ⊛ Ladbroke Grove, Notting Hill Gate

CONTEMPORARY APPLIED ARTS

www.caa.org.uk
For quality contemporary crafts, head to CAA, which is dedicated to promoting British artists.
✚ N6 ✉ 89 Southwark Street, SE1 ☎ 020 7436 2344 ⊙ Tue–Sat 10–6, Sun 11–5 ⊛ Southwark, Borough

DESIGNERS GUILD

www.designersguild.com
Tricia Guild's store is a wonderland of exquisite design, with a range of modern china, glass and fabrics.
✚ Off map ✉ 277 King's Road, SW3 ☎ 020 7351 5775 ⊙ Mon–Sat 10–6, Sun 12–5 ⊛ Sloane Square, then a 15 min walk or bus 19 or 22

FORBIDDEN PLANET

www.forbiddenplanet.com
This megastore sells a wide range of fantasy, horror and science fiction, as well as comic books.
✚ J4 ✉ 179 Shaftesbury Avenue, WC2 ☎ 020 7420 3666 ⊙ Daily ⊛ Tottenham Court Road

FORTNUM & MASON

www.fortnumandmason.com
Before venturing into London's premier grocer's shop, do not miss the clock, which has Messrs. Fortnum and Mason mincing forward each hour. The shop-brand Fortnum's goods make perfectly delicious presents.
✚ H6 ✉ 181 Piccadilly, W1 ☎ 0845 300 1707 ⊙ Mon–Sat 10–9, Sun 12–6 ⊛ Piccadilly Circus, Green Park

GRAYS ANTIQUE MARKET

www.graysantiques.com
High-quality goods ranging from silver to vintage fashion are sold by over 200 dealers.
✚ F5 ✉ 1–7 Davies Mews and 58 Davies Street, W1 ☎ 020 7629 7034 ⊙ Mon–Fri 10–6, Sat 11–5 ⊛ Bond Street

HAMLEYS

www.hamleys.com
In business for over 250 years and probably the world's most famous toy shop, Hamleys has five action-packed floors.
✚ H5 ✉ 188-196 Regent Street, W1 ☎ 0871 704 1977 ⊙ Daily Mon–Fri 10–9, Sat 9.30–9, Sun 12–6 ⊛ Oxford Circus

HARRODS
www.harrods.com
This vast emporium contains just about everything anyone could want. Don't miss the food halls.
➕ D8 ✉ 87–135 Brompton Road, SW1 ☎ 020 7730 1234 🕐 Daily Mon–Sat 10–8, Sun 11.30–6 🚇 Knightsbridge

HARVEY NICHOLS
www.harveynichols.com
Harvey Nichols bags the title of London's classiest clothes shop. It has a chic, popular restaurant.
➕ E7 ✉ 109–125 Knightsbridge, SW1 ☎ 020 7235 5000 🕐 Daily Mon–Sat 10–8, Sun 11.30–6 🚇 Knightsbridge

HATCHARDS
www.hatchards.co.uk
Hatchards' well-informed staff still know how to make book-buying a rewarding experience.
➕ H6 ✉ 187 Piccadilly, W1 ☎ 020 7439 9921 🕐 Daily 🚇 Piccadilly Circus, Green Park

HEAL'S
www.heals.co.uk
A front-runner of the 1920s Arts and Crafts movement, Heal's specializes in timeless contemporary furniture and homewares.
➕ J3 ✉ 196 Tottenham Court Road, W1 ☎ 020 7636 1666 🕐 Mon–Sat 10–7, Thu 10–8, Sun 12–6 🚇 Goodge Street

JIMMY CHOO
www.jimmychoo.com
A fashionista heaven, Jimmy Choo in Knightsbridge is the place to buy the highest-heeled shoes in town.
➕ E7 ✉ 32 Sloane Street, SW3 ☎ 020 7823 1051 🕐 Mon–Sat 10–5.30, Sun 12–5 🚇 Knightsbridge

LEADENHALL MARKET
www.leadenhallmarket.co.uk
This surprising City treat is housed under architect Horace Jones's 19th-century arcades, with quality food shops and pubs.
➕ R4 ✉ Leadenhall, EC3 🕐 Mon–Fri 10–5 🚇 Bank, Monument

Vibrant Camden Lock Market

AUCTION HOUSES
A visit to one of London's auction houses, even just to view, is an experience: try Bonham's (✉ 101 New Bond Street, W1 ☎ 020 7447 7447; www.bonhams.com), Christie's (✉ 8 King Street, SW1 ☎ 020 7839 9060; www.christies.com) or Sotheby's (✉ 34 New Bond Street, W1 ☎ 020 7293 5000; www.sothebys.com).

MAKE A PICNIC

With so many parks and benches, London is a great place to picnic. The big stores have seductive food halls and stock wine; see Harrods, Selfridges and Fortnum & Mason. Old Compton Street is a food shopper's delight; see also Clarke's Bakery (✉ 122 Kensington Church Street, W8) and other cafés that sell pre-prepared food to take out.

LIBERTY

www.liberty.co.uk

With everything from sumptuous fabrics to china and glass, this shop is characterized by exoticism and cutting-edge fashion, with an Arts and Crafts heritage, all in a beautiful mock-Tudor building.

➕ G4 ✉ Regent Street, W1 ☎ 020 7734 1234 🕐 Mon–Sat 10–8, Sun 12–6 🚇 Oxford Circus

LULU GUINNESS

www.luluguinness.com

Selling 1950s-style handbags, hats and shoes, this sleek, modern shop is popular with celebrities. Also in Burlington Arcade and in the City's Royal Exchange.

➕ E9 ✉ 3 Ellis Street, SW1 ☎ 020 7823 4828 🕐 Mon–Sat 10–6 🚇 Sloane Square

NEAL'S YARD REMEDIES

www.nealsyardremedies.com

Committed to using natural ingredients in its products, Neal's Yard health and beauty shop is a Covent Garden institution.

➕ K4 ✉ 15 Neal's Yard, WC2 ☎ 020 7379 7222 🕐 Mon–Sat 10–7, Sun 11–6 🚇 Covent Garden

PETER JONES

www.johnlewis.com

Shopping in this department store is a pleasure. There are great views from the café and cocktail bar.

➕ E9 ✉ Sloane Square, SW1 ☎ 0844 693 1751 🕐 Mon–Sat 9.30–7, Sun 10–6 🚇 Sloane Square

PETTICOAT LANE

Petticoat Lane is the place to go if you're looking for clothing at bargain prices. It is best on Sunday.

➕ S4 ✉ Middlesex and Wentworth streets, E1 🕐 Mon–Fri 8–4, Sun 9–2 🚇 Liverpool Street, Aldgate

ROCOCO

www.rococochocolates.com

The chocolates at this upscale chocolatier offer a taste sensation. Try the bars flavoured with Earl Grey tea, chilli pepper or nutmeg.

➕ Off map ✉ 321 King's Road, SW3 ☎ 020 7352 5857 🕐 Mon–Sat 10–6.30, Sun 11–6 🚇 Sloane Square

ROYAL EXCHANGE

William Tite's City landmark is now a beautiful upscale shopping mall.

➕ Q4 ✉ Cornhill 🕐 Mon–Fri, times vary from shop to shop 🚇 Bank

SELFRIDGES

www.selfridges.com

The main rival to Harvey Nichols (▷ 125) for daylong retail therapy. Don't miss the superb food hall.

➕ F4 ✉ 400 Oxford Street, W1 ☎ 0800 123 400 🕐 Daily 🚇 Marble Arch, Bond Street

SPITALFIELDS MARKET

www.visitspitalfields.co.uk

Wander among the craft stalls and array of food outlets. The Saturday Style Market attracts designers.

➕ S3 ✉ Crispin Place, E1 🕐 Mon–Fri 10–5, Sat 11–5, Sun 9–5 🚇 Liverpool Street

STANFORDS

www.stanfords.co.uk

With London's largest selection of maps, plus travel books and a good little café, Stanfords is a must for all travel enthusiasts.

➕ K5 ✉ 12–14 Long Acre, WC2 ☎ 020 7836 1321 🕔 Daily Ⓜ Covent Garden

THOMAS GOODE LTD

www.thomasgoode.com

Collectors of bone china need look no further than this splendid show-room. Famous English names include Wedgwood, Minton, Spode and Royal Worcester.

➕ F5 ✉ 19 South Audley Street, W1 ☎ 020 7499 2823 🕔 Mon–Sat 10–6 Ⓜ Green Park, Bond Street

TURNBULL & ASSER

www.turnbullandasser.co.uk

If you want classic British design, then the made-to-measure or off-the-peg shirts here are for you. Quality and service are superb.

➕ H6 ✉ 71–72 Jermyn Street, SW1 ☎ 020 7808 3000 🕔 Mon–Fri 9–6, Sat 9.30–6 Ⓜ Green Park, Piccadilly Circus

URBAN OUTFITTERS

www.urbanoutfitters.co.uk

Check out the latest trends in streetwear and accessories as well as unusual gifts and homewares.

➕ Off map ✉ 36–38 Kensington High Street, W8 ☎ 020 7761 1001 🕔 Daily Ⓜ High Street Kensington

VILLANDRY

www.villandry.com

This quality 'foodstore' sells French and English cheeses, great breads, olive oil, charcuterie and more.

➕ G3 ✉ 170 Great Portland Street, W1 ☎ 020 7631 3131 🕔 Daily Ⓜ Great Portland Street

SHOPPING SECRETS

For streets full of character, try Blenheim Crescent in Notting Hill, W11; Kensington Church Street, W8, renowned for its antiques shops and galleries; and village-like Marylebone High Street, W1, which delights with food, fashion, and Oxfam's flagship books and music shop. Secreted off Oxford Street, Gees Court and St. Christopher's Place are fashion favourites.

WESTFIELD LONDON

http://uk.westfield.com/london

With over 300 shops spanning designer and high-street labels, department stores and specialist boutiques, Westfield provides an all-day shopping experience. There are plenty of cafés and restaurants to sustain shoppers, too. The larger Westfield Stratford City is located by the Olympic site.

➕ Off map ✉ Ariel Way, W12 ☎ 020 3371 2300 Ⓜ Shepherd's Bush, Wood Lane

SHOP

Liberty's mock-Tudor main entrance

Entertainment

Once you've done with sightseeing for the day, you'll find lots of other great things to do with your time in this chapter, even if all you want to do is relax with a drink. In this section establishments are listed alphabetically.

ENTERTAINMENT

Introduction

When darkness falls, London's pace doesn't let up, and there's a huge choice of lively nightclubs, bars and pubs where you can mingle with the locals.

Entertainment

London's Theatreland, with its lavish West End musicals and plays starring A-list actors, is famed worldwide, but there's a great deal happening in smaller venues all over town, including alternative theatre, comedy and cabaret. Hundreds of concerts take place every week in a variety of buildings, but especially churches, where the quality of lunchtime and evening recitals is very high and admission is either nominal or free. London's newest cultural landmark is King's Place (☎ 020 7520 1440, www.kingsplace. co.uk) in the revitalized area of King's Cross. There are opera, ballet and modern dance seasons in memorable locations, too, plus an array of fun festivals, especially during the summer months and the long public holiday weekends.

Film

As well as the big-screen cinemas in the West End showing the latest blockbuster movies, London has some very good venues screening art-house and indie films. The BFI Southbank

---

WALK THE WALK

The 2km-long (1 mile) stretch of riverside on the South Bank between Westminster Bridge and London Bridge bustles by night, as well as by day. The London Eye is magical after dusk. On the opposite bank, illuminated landmarks include the Houses of Parliament and Somerset House. At Oxo Tower Wharf, go to the top floor for a drink or a meal—there are few better views of London. Admire Tate Modern (open until 10pm Friday and Saturday) and the Globe. Rest your feet at a riverside pub and enjoy spectacular views.

Clockwise from top: The Garrick Theatre in the West End; the Theatre Royal on Haymarket; the BFI IMAX on the South Bank; Shakespeare's Globe, a re-creation of

(▷ 133), which hosts the annual London Film Festival in October, Ciné Lumière (▷ 134), the Electric Cinema in Notting Hill (www.electriccinema.co.uk), the Curzon Mayfair and Renoir in the Brunswick Centre (both www.curzoncinemas.com) are all well worth visiting.

Summer Living

In the summer, London's outdoors comes into its own. Londoners enjoy concerts in beautiful settings such as Hampton Court Palace, Kenwood House, Hyde Park and Kew Gardens, often bringing picnics with them. The music ranges from classical and opera to jazz and rock. Bars, pubs and cafés spill onto the city's streets, and many serve good food.

Clubs, Pubs and Bars

Year-round, the diversity of the club scene is legendary, and with many changing themes, check before you go. There are tried-and-tested venues and a host of pulsing new wave options. London's extensive bar scene ranges from cocktails at the elegant Savoy (▷ 159) or the see-and-be-seen Blue Bar at The Berkeley (▷ 156) to Irish bars, sports bars and traditional street-corner pubs. You'll find some are in warrens of Tudor rooms; others take pride in their Victorian and Edwardian decorations.

LANDMARK CLUBBING

A mix of global names, trailblazing bands and DJs make Xoyo (✉ 32–37 Cowper Street, EC2 ☎ 020 7354 9993; www.xoyo.co.uk) a popular Shoreditch venue. The Nest (✉ 36–44 Stoke Newington Road, N16; www.ilovethenest.com) promises a soundtrack that covers everything from house and garage to disco, techno and trap from cutting-edge new talent. Under Blackfriars Bridge, Pulse (✉ Invicta Plaza, SE1 ☎ 020 7261 0981; www.pulseclub.co.uk) is London's largest state-of-the-art club space, with signature hi-tech sound and video mapping.

an Elizabethan playhouse; Young Dancer, *a bronze by Enzo Plazzotta outside the Royal Opera House in Covent Garden; jazz musicians play in the popular Dover Street*

Directory

South Bank

Clubs
Ministry of Sound
Film
BFI IMAX
BFI Southbank
Opera, Ballet and Concerts
Purcell Room
Queen Elizabeth Hall
Royal Festival Hall
Theatres
National Theatre
Old Vic
Shakespeare's Globe
Young Vic

Fleet Street to the Tower

Clubs
Fabric
Events
Broadgate Centre
Opera, Ballet and Concerts
Barbican Concert Hall
Theatres
Barbican Centre Theatre

Covent Garden to Regent's Park

Clubs
The Borderline
Guanabara
Salsa!
Jazz
Jazz After Dark
Pizza Express Jazz Club Soho
Smollensky's on the Strand
Opera, Ballet and Concerts
London Coliseum
Royal Opera House
Wigmore Hall
Theatres
Donmar Warehouse
Theatre Royal, Drury Lane

Westminster to St. James's

Bars
Trader Vic's
Clubs
Dover Street
Comedy
The Comedy Store
Dancing
The Ritz
Film
Institute of Contemporary Arts (ICA)
Opera, Ballet and Concerts
St. James's, Piccadilly
St. Martin-in-the-Fields

Around Hyde Park

Film
Ciné Lumière
Opera, Ballet and Concerts
Cadogan Hall
Holland Park Theatre
Royal Albert Hall
Theatres
Royal Court/Jerwood Theatre Upstairs

Further Afield

Clubs
606 Club
Barfly
Bush Hall
Koko
Notting Hill Arts Club
O2 Academy Brixton
Scala
Events
O2 Arena
Wembley
Jazz
Bull's Head, Barnes
Jazz Café
Opera, Ballet and Concerts
Sadler's Wells Theatre
Sport
All England Lawn Tennis Club, Wimbledon
Kia Oval
Lord's Cricket Ground
Wembley

Entertainment A–Z

606 CLUB
www.606club.co.uk
West London's best small jazz club books musicians with impeccable credentials. Alcohol is served only with food and the music cover charge is added to the cost of the meal.

Off map ✉ 90 Lots Road, SW10 ☎ 020 7352 5953 🕐 Mon–Thu 7pm–1am, Fri–Sat 8pm–2am, Sun 7–11pm 🚇 Earl's Court then bus C3, Fulham Broadway

ALL ENGLAND LAWN TENNIS CLUB, WIMBLEDON
www.wimbledon.com
In late June, line up for tickets to tennis's top tournament (advance tickets only for the last four days). Tours and museum entrance are available all year.

Off map ✉ Church Road, SW19 ☎ Tours: 020 8946 6131 🚇 Southfields

BARBICAN CENTRE THEATRE
www.barbican.org.uk
Currently an exciting mix of domestic and international companies play seasons here.

P3 ✉ Barbican Centre, Silk Street, EC2 ☎ 020 7638 8891 🚇 Barbican

BARBICAN CONCERT HALL
www.barbican.org.uk.
Home to the London Symphony Orchestra and the BBC Symphony Orchestra, the Barbican also welcomes visiting orchestras, singers and soloists.

R3 ✉ Barbican Centre, Silk Street, EC2 ☎ 020 7638 8891; range of good ticket deals 🚇 Barbican

BARFLY
www.barflyclub.com
A Camden club that hosts more than 20 indie groups a week—some bad, some OK and some destined for stardom.

Off map ✉ 49 Chalk Farm Road, NW1 ☎ 020 7424 0800 🕐 Mon–Thu 3pm–midnight, Fri–Sat 3pm–3am, Sun 7pm–midnight 🚇 Chalk Farm

BFI IMAX
www.bfi.org.uk/imax
Watch exhilarating 2-D and 3-D movies in this 500-seat cinema in a space-age setting.

L6 ✉ 1 Charlie Chaplin Walk, South Bank, SE1 ☎ 0330 333 7878 🚇 Embankment, Waterloo

BFI SOUTHBANK
www.bfi.org.uk
BFI Southbank screens a diverse range of films and is the focus of the annual London Film Festival.

L6 ✉ South Bank, SE1 ☎ 020 7928 3232 🚇 Embankment, Waterloo

THE BORDERLINE
http://theborderline.co.uk
The hottest indie and rock bands strut their stuff at the venerable Borderline club in the West End.

J4 ✉ Orange Yard, off Manette Street, W1 ☎ 020 7734 5547 🕐 Club: Mon–Wed 11pm–3am, Thu–Sat 11pm–4am. Shows: 7pm–10.30pm 🚇 Tottenham Court Road

---

THEATRE TIPS

If you care about where you sit, go in person and peruse the plan. For an evening 'sold out' performance, it is worth waiting in line for returns; otherwise, try for a matinée. The most inexpensive seats may be far from the stage or uncomfortable, so take binoculars and a cushion. Londoners rarely dress up for the theatre any more but they do order their intermission drinks before the play starts, and remain seated while they applaud.

The famed Comedy Store

BROADGATE CENTRE

www.broadgate.co.uk
This amphitheatre, surrounded by bars, restaurants and shops, provides a schedule of summer entertainment and a winter ice rink.
🕂 R3 ✉ Broadgate Circus, Eldon Street, EC2 ☎ 020 7505 5310 🚇 Liverpool Street

BULL'S HEAD, BARNES

www.thebullshead.com
Enjoy good jazz in the friendly atmosphere of a riverside pub.
🕂 Off map ✉ 373 Lonsdale Road, SW13 ☎ 020 8876 5241 🕙 Mon–Sun 12–11.30. Check website for jazz dates 🚉 Barnes Bridge

BUSH HALL

www.bushhallmusic.co.uk
Listen to jazz, rock, folk or classics performed by famous names and upcoming artists at this ornate Edwardian dance hall.
🕂 Off map ✉ 310 Uxbridge Road, Shepherd's Bush, W12 ☎ 020 8222 6955 🕙 Shows: 7.30pm, see website for listings 🚇 Shepherd's Bush Market

CADOGAN HALL

www.cadoganhall.com
This concert hall off Sloane Square is home to the Royal Philharmonic Orchestra. It also welcomes visiting musicians and vocalists.
🕂 E9 ✉ 5 Sloane Terrace, SW1 ☎ 020 7730 4500 🚇 Sloane Square

CINÉ LUMIÈRE

www.institut-francais.org.uk
Part of the French government's hub of language and culture, Ciné Lumière shows French films and other European and world cinema.
🕂 B9 ✉ Institut Français, 17 Queensberry Place, SW7 ☎ 020 7871 3535 🕙 Closed Aug 🚇 South Kensington

THE COMEDY STORE

www.thecomedystore.co.uk
The best in stand-up comedy features improvised sketches from the Comedy Store Players. Many big names in British TV and radio have cut their teeth here.
🕂 J5 ✉ 1a Oxendon Street, SW1 ☎ 0844 871 7699 🕙 Doors open Mon–Thu at 6.30pm, Fri–Sun 6pm. Show times vary, check website for details 🚇 Piccadilly Circus, Leicester Square

DONMAR WAREHOUSE

www.donmarwarehouse.com

The Donmar Warehouse attracts adventurous theatregoers to its avant-garde productions.

➕ J4 ✉ 41 Earlham Street, WC2 ☎ 0844 871 7624 🚇 Covent Garden

DOVER STREET

www.doverstreet.co.uk

Music at this large, popular basement, bedecked with candles, can be jump jive, jazz, latin, soul, swing or funk. The food is good. Dress code is smart casual.

➕ G6 ✉ 8–10 Dover Street, W1 ☎ 020 7629 9813 🍴 Restaurant: Mon–Thu 6.30pm–3am, Fri–Sat 7pm–3am. Club: Mon–Sat 10pm–3am 🚇 Piccadilly Circus, Green Park

FABRIC

www.fabriclondon.com

This fabulously cool superclub is known for its music blasted out in three rooms and is hugely popular.

➕ N3 ✉ 77a Charterhouse Street, EC1 ☎ 020 7336 8898 🍴 Sat–Sun 11pm–8am, Fri 10pm–6am 🚇 Farringdon

GUANABARA

www.guanabara.co.uk

Grab a *caipirinha* and salsa onto the dance floor at this Brazilian-themed venue. Tables must be booked in advance.

➕ K4 ✉ Parker Street, WC2 ☎ 020 7242 8600 🍴 Mon–Sat 5pm–2.30am, Sun 5pm–midnight 🚇 Covent Garden, Holborn

HOLLAND PARK THEATRE

www.operahollandpark.com

Confusingly, this is highly acclaimed opera, not theatre, staged in summer (June to August) beneath a canopy in one of London's most romantic parks.

➕ Off map ✉ Holland Park, W8 ☎ 020 7361 3570 🚇 Holland Park, High Street Kensington

INSTITUTE OF CONTEMPORARY ARTS (ICA)

www.ica.org.uk

Founded by a collective of artists, poets and writers, the Institute of Contemporary Arts hosts cutting-edge art, screens seriously arty films and plays host to performance artists charting new territory in all media.

➕ J6 ✉ The Mall, SW1 ☎ 020 7930 3647 🚇 Piccadilly Circus, Charing Cross

JAZZ AFTER DARK

www.jazzafterdark.co.uk

Jazz and blues attract a keen young crowd. The cocktails are good and the food simple.

➕ J4 ✉ 9 Greek Street, W1 ☎ 020 7734 0545 🍴 Mon–Thu 5pm–2am, Fri–Sat 5pm–3am 🚇 Tottenham Court Road

JAZZ CAFÉ

www.jazzcafelive.com

Buzzing nightly with the widest range of jazz, from soul to rap, this is a popular spot for the young.

➕ Off map ✉ 5 Parkway, NW1 ☎ 020 7688 8899 (restaurant); 0844 847 2514 (tickets) 🍴 Mon–Sun 7pm–2am 🚇 Camden Town

ALL THAT JAZZ

London has a great concentration of world-class jazz musicians, both home-grown and foreign, traditional and contemporary. Evening and late-night gigs cover rock, roots, rhythm and blues and more, many in pubs. For a list of venues, check *Time Out*. Also, to get the latest information on jazz visit www.jazznights.co.uk.

KIA OVAL

www.kiaoval.com

The Oval is where Surrey County Cricket Club play home games. It is also a venue for test cricket and Sunday league games.

Off map ✉ Surrey County Cricket Club, Kennington, SE11 ☎ 0844 375 1845 Oval

KOKO

www.koko.uk.com

Since 1890, this Camden Town venue has been through many incarnations. Today, go for hip-hop, trance, pop, rock and partying under the gigantic mirror ball.

Off map ✉ 1a Camden High Street, NW1 ☎ 0870 432 5527 Sun–Thu 7pm–11.30pm, Fri 7pm–9.30pm. Club NME: Fri 9.30pm–4am, Sat 9pm–4am Mornington Crescent, Camden Town

LONDON COLISEUM

www.eno.org

The London Coliseum is home to the English National Opera (ENO), which is known for its exciting and innovative productions.

J5 ✉ St. Martin's Lane, WC2 ☎ 020 7845 9300 Leicester Square, Charing Cross

TICKET TIPS

Use the 'tkts' half-price ticket booth (in Leicester Square). Preview tickets and matinée tickets have reduced prices. Get up early and line up for one-day bargain tickets at the RNT and RSC. Go with friends and make a party booking at a reduced rate. Ask the National Theatre, Royal Court and other theatres about special discounts on particular performances; and keep student and senior citizen cards ready. Remember, the show is the same wherever you sit!

LORD'S CRICKET GROUND

www.lords.org

Lords is the home of the MCC (Marylebone Cricket Club) and is where Middlesex play home games. The ground hosts test cricket, major finals and Sunday league games.

Off map ✉ St. John's Wood Road, NW8 ☎ 020 7616 8500 St. John's Wood

MINISTRY OF SOUND

www.ministryofsound.com

This legendary club is housed in a prison-like building and stars world-class DJs.

N8 ✉ 103 Gaunt Street, SE1 ☎ 0870 060 0010 7378 Fri 10.30pm–6am, Sat 11pm–7am (last entry 4.30am) Elephant and Castle

NATIONAL THEATRE

www.nationaltheatre.org.uk

Home of the National Theatre company, there are three performance spaces; the Olivier, Lyttelton and Cottesloe. All stage several productions in repertory.

L6 ✉ South Bank, SE1 ☎ 020 7452 3000 Information, tickets and tours Embankment, Waterloo Waterloo

NOTTING HILL ARTS CLUB

www.nottinghillartsclub.com

Diversity and originality results from artists and DJs meeting here and swapping ideas.

Off map ✉ 21 Notting Hill Gate, W11 ☎ 020 7598 5226 Times vary, check website for details Notting Hill Gate

O2 ACADEMY BRIXTON

www.o2academybrixton.co.uk

South London's favourite live music venue attracts big-name bands. It has an art deco interior and room for nearly 5,000 on the huge sloping dance floor. All the big rock bands have played and recorded here.

➕ Off map ✉ 211 Stockwell Road, SW9 ☎ 020 7771 3000 ⏰ Times vary, check website for details 🚇 Brixton, Stockwell

O2 ARENA

www.theo2.co.uk

A music and sports venue in former Millennium Dome, the O2 Arena has a capacity of 20,000.

➕ Off map ✉ Peninsula Square, SE10 ☎ 0844 856 0202 🚇 North Greenwich

OLD VIC

www.oldvictheatre.com

This sumptuous theatre stages critically acclaimed productions.

➕ M7 ✉ The Cut, Waterloo Road, SE1 ☎ 0844 871 7628 🚇 Waterloo, Southwark

PIZZA EXPRESS JAZZ CLUB SOHO

www.pizzaexpresslive.com

Savour quality pizzas and great jazz in this friendly Soho cellar (booking essential).

➕ J4 ✉ 10 Dean Street, W1 ☎ 0845 6027 017 🚇 Tottenham Court Road

PURCELL ROOM

www.southbankcentre.co.uk

Listen to chamber music, singers and musicians and more in this intimate space.

➕ L6 ✉ South Bank, SE1 ☎ 0844 875 0073 🚇 Embankment, Waterloo

QUEEN ELIZABETH HALL

www.southbankcentre.co.uk

Come here for small orchestras, choirs, small-scale opera, piano recitals and dance.

➕ L6 ✉ South Bank, SE1 ☎ 0844 875 0073 🚇 Embankment, Waterloo

THE RITZ

www.theritzlondon.com

To enter a bygone world, dress up for dinner and a dance on a Friday or Saturday at London's most opulent dining room (booking essential). For a more modest experience, go for afternoon tea or to the Rivoli Bar.

➕ G6 ✉ 150 Piccadilly, W1 ☎ 020 7493 8181 🚇 Green Park

ROYAL ALBERT HALL

www.royalalberthall.com

Sporting events fill the 6,000-seat hall as successfully as the annual 'Prom' season (the Henry Wood Promenade Concerts), which runs from mid-July to mid-September, offering nightly concerts and cheap 'prom' tickets to stand or sit on the floor of the pit.

➕ B7 ✉ Kensington Gore, SW7 ☎ 0845 401 5045 🚇 South Kensington

ROYAL COURT/JERWOOD THEATRE UPSTAIRS

www.royalcourttheatre.com

The Royal Court has a lofty artistic reputation and presents only new work by leading or emerging playwrights. In the 1950s, John Osbourne's *Look Back In Anger* shook up London theatre forever, and today's productions follow in its wake. The main theatre seats 400, the studio 60.

🞦 E9 ✉ Sloane Square, SW1 ☎ 020 7565 5000 Ⓜ Sloane Square

ROYAL FESTIVAL HALL

www.southbankcentre.co.uk
The Royal Festival Hall, at the heart of the South Bank Centre arts complex, stages world-class performances, with large-scale orchestral concerts, plus jazz and ballet.

🞦 L6 ✉ South Bank, SE1 ☎ 0844 875 0073 Ⓜ Embankment, Waterloo

ROYAL OPERA HOUSE

www.roh.org.uk
The opulent Royal Opera House in Covent Garden is home to the Royal Ballet and is an evocative setting for grand opera.

🞦 K5 ✉ Bow Street, Covent Garden, WC2 ☎ 020 7304 4000 Ⓜ Covent Garden

SADLER'S WELLS THEATRE

www.sadlerswells.com
Sadler's Wells is one of the most electrifying dance theatres in Europe, with international and British companies presenting innovative dance of all genres.

🞦 M1 ✉ Rosebery Avenue, EC1 ☎ 020 7863 8198 Ⓜ Angel

ST. JAMES'S, PICCADILLY

www.spj.org.uk
Sir Christopher Wren's mid-17th-century church makes a sumptuous setting for lunchtime and evening choral and orchestral concerts, plus star lecturers.

🞦 H6 ✉ 197 Piccadilly, W1 ☎ 020 7734 4511 Ⓜ Piccadilly Circus

ST. MARTIN-IN-THE-FIELDS

www.stmartin-in-the-fields.org
Baroque music is the focus of the free lunchtime concerts (Monday, Tuesday and Friday) and candlelit evening concerts (Thursday, Friday and Saturday). There are also jazz nights in the crypt, where there's a popular, good-value café/restaurant.

🞦 K5 ✉ Trafalgar Square, WC2 ☎ 020 7766 1100 Ⓜ Leicester Square

SALSA!

www.bar-salsa.com
Come here for a salsa class held in the bar, then dance the night away or enjoy great Latin American food.

🞦 J5 ✉ 96 Charing Cross Road, WC2 ☎ 020 7379 3277 🕔 Sun–Thu 5pm–2am, Fri–Sat 5pm–3am Ⓜ Tottenham Court Road

SCALA

www.scala-london.co.uk
This King's Cross superclub is spread over four main floors, with a viewing gallery. Music is provided by DJs and live bands.

📍 Off map ✉ Pentonville Road, N1
☎ 020 7833 2022 🕐 Live music nights:
7.30pm–11pm. Club nights: 9pm–3am
🚇 King's Cross

SHAKESPEARE'S GLOBE
www.shakespearesglobe.com
The performance season at this
reconstruction of an open-air
Elizabethan playhouse runs May to
September; take a coat and rainhat
to watch works by Shakespeare
and his contemporaries. Tours
operate year-round (▷ 46).
📍 P6 ✉ 21 New Globe Walk, SE1
☎ 020 7401 9919 🚇 London Bridge,
Mansion House, Blackfriars, Southwark

A production at Shakespeare's Globe

SMOLLENSKY'S ON THE STRAND
www.smollenskys.com
A pianist plays on week nights and
there is jazz on Sunday nights at
this American bar and grill that
opened in 1986.
📍 K5 ✉ 105 The Strand, WC2 ☎ 020
7497 2101 🚇 Charing Cross

THEATRE ROYAL, DRURY LANE
www.theatre-royaldrurylane.com
The theatre, built in 1812, stages
mostly musicals. It is believed to
be haunted—the Man in Grey is
said to walk around the Upper
Circle.
📍 K5 ✉ Catherine Street, WC2 ☎ 0844
871 8810 🚇 Covent Garden

TRADER VIC'S
www.tradervicslondon.com
The South Seas meet Park Lane in
this Tahitian-inspired bar in the
Hilton Hotel. It's pricey but fun, and
the tropical cocktails are a work of
art. The bar is open daily.
📍 F6 ✉ 22 Park Lane, W1 ☎ 020 7208
4113 🚇 Hyde Park Corner

WEMBLEY
www.wembleystadium.com
www.livenation.co.uk/wembley
The state-of-the art football
stadium, where the English
national team plays home games,
also hosts big-name pop and rock
concerts.
📍 Off map ✉ Stadium Way, Wembley,
Middlesex ☎ 0844 980 8001 🚇 Wembley
Park 🚆 Wembley Stadium

WIGMORE HALL
www.wigmore-hall.org.uk
The hall was built in 1901 as a
recital hall for Bechstein Pianos, so
it has perfect acoustics. It is one of
London's most beautiful settings
for recitals and chamber music,
especially for Sunday concerts.
📍 F4 ✉ 36 Wigmore Street, W1
☎ 020 7935 2141 🚇 Bond Street

YOUNG VIC
www.youngvic.org
Young directors stage innovative
productions of classic and new
plays and musicals here.
📍 M7 ✉ The Cut, SE1 ☎ 020 7922 2922
🚇 Waterloo, Southwark

Eat

There are places to eat across the city to suit all tastes and budgets. In this section establishments are listed alphabetically.

EAT

Introduction

With more than 50 restaurants awarded one or more Michelin stars, the capital's reputation for fine dining continues to grow. Chefs have high profiles and London creates its own culinary trends. Using the finest-quality ingredients, modern British cuisine values simplicity and flavour, innovation and elegant presentation.

Cafés, Brasseries and Pubs
Multicultural London offers exciting restaurants serving a wide variety of different cuisines, ranging from European and cutting-edge contemporary to Indian, Asian and Middle Eastern. Tapas and sushi bars are popular and you don't have to look far to find a good spicy curry or fragrant Thai treat. No longer just an excuse to rest your feet, museum and art gallery cafés are as much of a destination as their exhibitions and, with their all-day menus, convivial brasseries have a relaxed Continental air. Gastropubs combine a fine setting with quality drinks and food.

Fast Food and Restaurant Chains
Try the Gourmet Burger Kitchen, Yo!Sushi, Wagamama, All-Bar-One and Masala Zone. Zizzi and Pizza Express are good pizza chains.

Afternoon Tea
A great British institution, afternoon tea is still available in hotels and tearooms from about 2 or 3pm. It always includes a pot of tea and something to eat, which can vary from dainty sandwiches and cakes to scones with clotted cream and jam.

DRESS CODE

In the past the British loved to dress for dinner, but these days only the most formal restaurants demand a jacket and tie. Customers should dress appropriately, however, to eat in upscale restaurants.

Top to bottom: The Palm Court at the Ritz; summertime alfresco dining in the capital; focaccia for sale at Borough Market; artisan breads, Borough Market

Directory

South Bank

British and Modern
Oxo Tower Bar,
  Brasserie &
  Restaurant
European
Baltic
Cantina Vinopolis
Gastropubs/Bars
The Anchor
Anchor & Hope
Lighter Bites
Tate Modern Café

Fleet Street to the Tower

British and Modern
Cicada
Medcalf
St. John
European
Bevis Marks
  Restaurant
Club Gascon
Famous Chefs
Fifteen
Rhodes Twenty Four
Fish and Vegetarian
The Café Below
Gastropubs/Bars
The Peasant

Covent Garden to Regent's Park

Asian
Benares
Chaopraya Eat-Thai
Imli Street
Masala Zone
Rasa W1
Brasseries/Brunch
Christopher's
Joe Allen
British and Modern
Rules

European
Gaby's Deli
Hibiscus
Villandry
Wild Honey
Famous Chefs
The Square
Fish and Vegetarian
Wild Food Café
Gastropubs/Bars
Detroit
Lowlander
International
Ceviche
Lighter Bites
Paul

Westminster and St. James's

Asian
Tamarind
British and Modern
Portrait Restaurant
The Wolseley
Famous Chefs
Le Gavroche
Greenhouse
International
Gaucho
Lighter Bites
Inn the Park

Around Hyde Park

Asian
Amaya
Royal China
British and Modern
Babylon
Le Café Anglais
Maggie Jones's
Famous Chefs
Maze
Tom Aikens
Lighter Bites
The Orangery

Further Afield

British and Modern
The Glasshouse
Ottolenghi
European
La Poule au Pot
Providores & Tapa
  Room
Gastropubs/Bars
The Gun

Eating A–Z

PRICES

Prices are approximate, based on a 3-course meal for one person.

£££	over £60
££	£30–£60
£	under £30

AMAYA ££

www.amaya.biz

Enjoy sophisticated Indian grills and curries in an upscale setting with a theatrical show kitchen.

➕ E8 ✉ Halkin Arcade, SW1 ☎ 020 7823 1166 ⏰ Mon–Sat 12.30–2.15, 6.30–11.30, Sun 12.45–2.45, 6.30–10.30 🚇 Knightsbridge

THE ANCHOR £

This historic pub with black beams, a maze of tiny rooms and garden terrace enjoys excellent river views. Food is traditional British, with fish and chips and Sunday roasts.

➕ P6 ✉ Bankside, 34 Park Street, SE1 ☎ 020 7407 1577 ⏰ Restaurant: Mon–Sat 12–10, Sun 12–9 🚇 London Bridge

RIVERSIDE EATING

London is exploiting the potential of its riverside views. As well as traditional pubs such as The Anchor (▷ above) many new restaurants are opening along the South Bank. The most spectacular views are from the Oxo Tower Restaurant (▷ 149) and Tate Modern's rooftop restaurant at Bankside (▷ 151). There are lower but impressive views from the collection of eateries that line the Thames in the Southbank Centre (▷ 83). For a more modest river view, try the Narrow pub (✉ 44 Narrow Street, E14), which overlooks the wider, curving Thames of the East End.

ANCHOR & HOPE ££

A quality gastropub in a great building, the Anchor & Hope serves good British food. There are no reservations, so arrive early. Service can be slow.

➕ M7 ✉ 36 The Cut, SE1 ☎ 020 7928 9898 ⏰ Tue–Sat 11–11, Mon 5–11, Sun 12.30–5 🚇 Southwark, Waterloo

BABYLON ££

www.roofgardens.virgin.com

Take a seat in the amazing rooftop gardens, complete with oak trees, flamingos and expansive views over London, for elegant modern British cuisine. Being there is a great experience.

➕ Off map ✉ The Roof Garden, 99 Kensington High Street, W8 ☎ 020 7368 3993 ⏰ Mon–Sat 12–2.30, 7–10.30, Sun 12–4 🚇 High Street Kensington

BALTIC £

www.balticrestaurant.co.uk

Head to the bar for some serious cocktails, then on to the dramatic contemporary restaurant for modern Polish and Eastern European food and jazz every Sunday 7pm.

➕ N6 ✉ 74 Blackfriars Road, SE1 ☎ 020 7928 1111 ⏰ Restaurant: Mon–Sat 5.30–11.15, Tue–Sat lunch 12–3, Sun 12–4.30, 5.30–10.30. Bar: 12–12 🚇 Southwark

BENARES £££

www.benaresrestaurant.com

Atul Kochhar serves subtly spiced and stylishly presented Indian dishes in his Michelin-starred Mayfair restaurant. The menu is seasonally inspired, with innovative vegetarian options.

➕ G5 ✉ 12a Berkeley Square House, Berkeley Square, W1 ☎ 020 7629 8886 ⏰ Daily 12–2.30, Mon–Sat 12–2.30, 5.30–11 🚇 Green Park

BEVIS MARKS RESTAURANT ££

www.bevismarkstherestaurant.com

You'll find elegant dining at this highly rated kosher restaurant, with Israeli and other wines on offer.

➕ R4 ⊠ 3 Middlesex Street, E1 ☎ 020 7283 2220 🕔 Mon–Fri 12–3, Mon–Thu 5.30–10.30 🚇 Aldgate

LE CAFÉ ANGLAIS £–££

www.lecafeanglais.co.uk

Rowley Leigh's vast but inviting art deco restaurant in the Whiteley's shopping centre attracts food-lovers with an unfussy menu, an open kitchen and oyster bar.

➕ A4 ⊠ 8 Porchester Gardens, W2 ☎ 020 7221 1415 🕔 Restaurant: Mon–Thu 12–3.30, 6.30–10.30, Fri–Sat 12–3.30, 6.30–11, Sun 12–3.30, 6.30–10. Oyster Bar: Mon–Sat 12–10.30, Sun 12–5 🚇 Bayswater, Queensway

THE CAFÉ BELOW £

www.cafebelow.co.uk

Exceptional vegetarian food is served in this ancient Norman church crypt. It serves lunch only.

➕ P4 ⊠ St. Mary-le-Bow, Cheapside, EC2 ☎ 020 7329 0789 🕔 Mon–Fri 7.30am–2.30pm 🚇 Bank, St. Paul's, Mansion House

CANTINA VINOPOLIS ££

www.cantinavinopolis.com

At this wine-themed restaurant, Mediterranean-influenced dishes are prepared in an open kitchen.

➕ P6 ⊠ 1 Bank End, SE1 ☎ 020 7940 8333 🕔 Mon–Wed 6pm–11pm, Thu–Fri 12–3, 6–11, Sat 12–11 🚇 London Bridge

CEVICHE £–££

www.cevicheuk.com

Peruvian food is the big new taste sensation and Ceviche is the hot London source of this tasty and healthy cuisine.

➕ J4 ⊠ 17 Frith Street, W1 ☎ 020 7292 2040 🕔 Mon–Sat 12–11.30, 6–11, Sun 12–10.15 🚇 Tottenham Court Road, Leicester Square, Piccadilly Circus

CHAOPRAYA EAT-THAI ££

www.eatthai.net

Enjoy classic Thai dishes at this quiet, stylish restaurant just behind Oxford Street.

➕ F4 ⊠ 22 St. Christopher's Place, W1 ☎ 020 7486 0777 🕔 Daily 12–3, 6–11 🚇 Bond Street

CHRISTOPHER'S ££

www.christophersgrill.com

One of the best places in London for a genuine American brunch, Christopher's is in a beautiful Victorian town house with a Martini Bar on the ground floor.

➕ K5 ⊠ 18 Wellington Street, WC2 ☎ 020 7240 4222 🕔 Mon–Wed 11.30am–midnight, Thu–Sat 11.30am–1am, Sun 11.30–10.30. Martini bar: Mon–Wed 11.30am–midnight, Thu–Sat 11.30am–1.30am 🚇 Covent Garden

EAT

Vegetarians are well-catered to in London. Most restaurants offer a range of meat-free meals, while Indian cooking is famed for its imaginative vegetable and pulse dishes. If fish remains an option, the capital has a wide range on offer.

CICADA £

www.rickerrestaurants.com

A popular minimalist bar/restaurant serving Pan-Asian fusion food including dim sum, curries, sashimi and salads, Cicada attracts a stylish crowd who create a lively, fun atmosphere.

🔲 N3 ⊠ 132–136 St. John Street, EC1 ☎ 020 7608 1550 🕘 Mon–Fri 12–11, Sat 6–11 🚇 Farringdon

CLUB GASCON £££

www.clubgascon.com

Good for that special dinner, Club Gascon serves unusual, robust dishes from Gascony. Reserve well in advance.

🔲 N3 ⊠ 57 West Smithfield, EC1 ☎ 020 7600 6144 🕘 Mon–Fri 12–2, 7–10, Sat 6.30–10.30 🚇 Barbican, Farringdon

DETROIT £

www.detroit-bar.com

Retro decor, funky sounds and tempting cocktails feature at this established Covent Garden bar. The bar snacks menu includes burgers, vegetable tempura and a trio of houmous.

🔲 K4 ⊠ 35 Earlham Street, WC2 ☎ 020 7240 2662 🕘 Mon–Sat 5–midnight 🚇 Leicester Square

FIFTEEN ££

www.fifteen.net

At Fifteen, popular TV chef Jamie Oliver provides successful training for the unemployed. The mainly Italian cuisine is served in the Trattoria and in the open-kitchen restaurant downstairs. Booking is advised.

🔲 Q1 ⊠ 15 Westland Place, N1 ☎ 020 3375 1515 🕘 Mon–Sun 12–3, 6–10 🚇 Old Street

GABY'S DELI £

Inspired by a New York Jewish diner, this is the place to head for no-nonsense food, either to eat in or take out.

A classic double-decker club sandwich served with flair
Modern British cuisine uses the finest ingredients

J5 ✉ 30 Charing Cross Road, WC2
☎ 020 7836 4233 🕔 Mon–Sat 9am–
midnight, Sun 12–10pm 🚇 Leicester
Square

GAUCHO £££

www.gauchorestaurants.co.uk
Meat-eaters will relish the steaks
at this Argentinian restaurant and
wine bar. Or for a lighter meal, try
the tasty *ceviches* (marinated raw
fish). Excellent South American
wines complement the food. The
top floor has live music.
H5 ✉ 25 Swallow Street, W1 ☎ 020
7734 4040 🕔 Mon–Sat 12–12, Sun 12–11
🚇 Piccadilly Circus

LE GAVROCHE £££

www.le-gavroche.co.uk
Albert's Roux's son sticks to classic
French cuisine, but creates lighter
dishes. Enjoy amazing wines and a
grand setting.
E5 ✉ 43 Upper Brook Street, W1
☎ 020 7408 0881 🕔 Mon–Fri 12–2,
6.30–11, Sat 6.30–11 🚇 Marble Arch

THE GLASSHOUSE £££

www.glasshouserestaurant.co.uk
The perfect preamble to a walk
in Kew Gardens or for a special
evening out, the Glasshouse
serves notable modern dishes,
beautifully presented. The owners
are passionate about wine, too,
so the list is impressive. Reserve
in advance.
Off map ✉ 14 Station Parade, Kew
☎ 020 8940 6777 🕔 Mon–Sat 12–2.30,
6.30–10.30, Sun 7–10 🚇 Kew Gardens

GREENHOUSE £££

www.greenhouserestaurant.co.uk
Chef Arnaud Bignon serves
imaginative yet serious food,
complemented by superb wines.

Choose from the à la carte,
seasonal, lunch or tasting menus
and enjoy fine contemporary
French cuisine that hasn't forgotten
its classic roots.
G6 ✉ 27a Hay's Mews, W1 ☎ 020
7499 3331 🕔 Mon–Fri 12–2.30, 6.30–11,
Sat 6.30–11 🚇 Green Park

THE GUN ££

www.thegundocklands.com
A popular, comfortable gastropub
on Canary Wharf, with stunning
views, The Gun serves imaginative,
seasonal British food. A typical
choice from the menu would be
the Brixham plaice with aromatic
English samphire, Jersey Royal
potatoes and *beurre noisette*.
Off map ✉ 27 Coldharbour, Isle of
Dogs, E14 ☎ 020 7515 5222
🕔 Mon–Sat 11am–midnight, Sun 11–11
🚇 Canary Wharf, Blackwall

HIBISCUS £££

www.hibiscusrestaurant.co.uk
Chef Claude Bosi's bold, inventive
modern French cooking never fails
to get rave reviews.
G5 ✉ 29 Maddox Street, W1S
☎ 020 7629 2999 🕔 Tue–Thu 12–2.30,
6.30–11, Fri–Sat 12–2.30, 6–11
🚇 Oxford Circus

EAT

The unmistakable OXO Tower

IMLI STREET £–££
www.imlistreet.com
Contemporary Indian dishes, inspired by street food and served tapas-style, is ideal for sharing.
🔲 H4 ✉ 167–169 Wardour Street, W1 ☎ 020 7287 4243 ⏰ Daily 8am–11pm 🚇 Tottenham Court Road

INN THE PARK £
www.peytonandbyrne.co.uk/inn-the-park
Enjoy inspired British food with lake and park views from the terrace. Tempting afternoon teas are served daily 3–4.30pm.
🔲 J7 ✉ St. James's Park, SW1 ☎ 020 7451 9999 ⏰ Daily 8–11 (9–11 Sat–Sun), 12–4.30, 5–11 🚇 St. James's Park

JOE ALLEN ££
www.joeallen.co.uk
For American food and beer head to this dependably convivial and clublike establishment. Reservations are essential.
🔲 K5 ✉ 13 Exeter Street, WC2 ☎ 020 7836 0651 ⏰ Mon–Thu 12–2, Fri noon–1am, Sun 10am–1am, Sun 12–12 🚇 Covent Garden

LOWLANDER £
www.lowlander.com
This Belgian bar and brasserie is in a great spot for a pre-theatre meal. Try the rib-eye *steak frites*.
🔲 K4 ✉ 36 Drury Lane, WC2 ☎ 020 7379 7446 ⏰ Mon–Fri 9.30am–11pm, Sat 9.30am–11.30pm, Sun 10am–10.30pm 🚇 Covent Garden

MAGGIE JONES'S ££
www.maggie-jones.co.uk
This cosy Kensington institution has been around for over 40 years and is much-loved for its informality, wine list and no-nonsense British food.
🔲 Off map ✉ 6 Old Court Place, Kensington Church Street, W8 ☎ 020 7937 6462 ⏰ Daily 12–2.30, 6–11 (Sun 10) 🚇 High Street Kensington

MASALA ZONE ££
www.masalazone.com
From the creators of Chutney Mary and Veeraswamy, both known for their authentic dishes, comes an informal setting for thalis and Indian street food. There are other branches in the capital.
🔲 H5 ✉ 9 Marshall Street, W1 ☎ 020 7287 9966 ⏰ Mon–Sat 12–11, Sun 12.30–10.30 🚇 Oxford Circus

---

SET-PRICE MENUS

Many of London's pricier restaurants offer two set-price menus—lower in price at lunchtime. Try classic Anglo-French cuisine at the Connaught Grill (🔲 E5 ✉ 16 Carlos Place, W1 ☎ 020 7107 8880) or lunch at Gordon Ramsey's Maze (▷ 149). Most of the star chefs offer these menus including Tom Aikins, Richard Corrigan and Philip Howard.

EAT

MAZE ££–£££

www.gordonramsay.com/maze

Enjoy Gordon Ramsay's imaginative haute cuisine—French with Asian influences—in a wonderfully congenial atmosphere. The three- and four-course lunchtime set menus are competitively priced.

🔲 F5 ✉ 10–13 Grosvenor Square, W1 ☎ 020 7107 0000 🕐 Daily 12–3, 6–11 🚇 Bond Street

MEDCALF £–££

www.medcalfbar.co.uk

The carefully crafted British menu changes daily and respects top-quality ingredients.

🔲 M2 ✉ 40 Exmouth Market, EC1 ☎ 020 7833 3533 🕐 Mon–Sat 12–3, 6–10, (Fri–10.30), Sun 12–3.30. Bar: Mon–Sat 12–11 (Fri 12), Sun 12–4 🚇 Farringdon

THE ORANGERY £

www.hrp.org.uk

An 18th-century building overlooking Kensington Palace's formal gardens creates the perfect setting for elegant light lunches or afternoon tea—cucumber sandwiches or scones with jam and cream.

🔲 A6 ✉ Kensington Palace, Kensington Gardens, W8 ☎ 020 3166 6113 🕐 Mar–Sep daily 10–6; Oct–Feb 10–5 🚇 High Street Kensington

OTTOLENGHI £

www.ottolenghi.co.uk

Merely looking at the restaurant is sustaining; eating here around the communal tables is even better. The Mediterranean-influenced dishes are fresh, colourful and full of flavour. Favourites include roast chicken with chilli and basil and roasted sweet potato with pecan and maple syrup. The restaurant is opposite the Almeida Theatre.

🔲 Off map ✉ 287 Upper Street, N1 ☎ 020 7288 1454 🕐 Mon–Sat 8am–10.30pm, Sun 9am–7pm 🚇 Angel, Highbury & Islington

OXO TOWER BAR, BRASSERIE AND RESTAURANT ££–£££

www.harveynichols.com

Look out over London while eating, drinking or snacking on good British and pan-Asian food. There are plenty of outdoor tables; reservations are essential.

🔲 M6 ✉ 8th Floor, Oxo Tower Wharf, Barge House Street, SE1 ☎ 020 7803 3888 🕐 Mon–Fri 12–2.30, 6–11, Sat 12–2.30, 5.30–11, Sun 12–3, 6.30–10 🚇 Blackfriars

PAUL £

www.paul-uk.com

This stunning patisserie is a branch of its French mother founded in 1889. Sample divine hot chocolate and pastries. There are more than 30 other branches across London.

🔲 K5 ✉ 29 Bedford Street, WC2 ☎ 020 7836 3304 🕐 Mon–Fri 7am–9pm, Sat–Sun 8am–9pm 🚇 Covent Garden

EAT

BUFFET DEALS

Unlimited food at a fixed price is practical for families with growing children—or simply for hungry adults. Many larger hotels do breakfast and lunch buffets, especially good on Sunday when many Indian restaurants do the same.

THE PEASANT £–££

www.thepeasant.co.uk

Expect a warm welcome at this north London gastropub. Classic and modern British food is served in the bar, with more sophisticated flavours on offer in the upstairs restaurant.

✚ N3 ✉ 240 St. John Street, EC1 ☎ 020 7336 7726 🕙 Mon–Sat 12–11, Sun 12–10.30 🚇 Farringdon

PORTRAIT RESTAURANT ££

www.searcys.co.uk

In this restaurant at the National Portrait Gallery every table benefits from the fine view. Try the salmon with cream sauce for a summer lunch. Reservations are essential.

✚ J5 ✉ National Portrait Gallery, St. Martin's Place, WC2 ☎ 020 7312 2490 🕙 Daily 10–11, 11.45–2.45, 3.30–4.45; Thu, Fri, Sat 5.30–8.15 🚇 Leicester Square, Charing Cross

LA POULE AU POT ££

www.pouleaupot.co.uk

A Belgravia institution, loved as much for its romantic, retro country atmosphere as its classic French cooking. Think bouillabaisse, boeuf bourguignon, cassoulet and tarte tatin. In summer, the outdoor terrace is popular for alfresco trysts.

✚ Off map at F9 ✉ 231 Ebury Street, SW1 ☎ 020 7730 7763 🕙 Mon–Fri 12–2.30, 6.45–11, Sat 12–4, 6.45–11, Sun 12–4, 6.45–10 🚇 Sloane Square

PROVIDORES & TAPA ROOM ££

www.theprovidores.co.uk

Enjoy imaginative dishes and New Zealand wines at this café, wine bar and fine dining restaurant.

✚ F3 ✉ 109 Marylebone High Street, W1 ☎ 020 7935 6175 🕙 Mon–Fri 9am–10.30pm, Sat 10am–10.30pm, Sun 10–10 🚇 Baker Street

RASA W1 £

www.rasarestaurants.com

One of several Rasa restaurants in the capital, Rasa W1 serves inspired cooking from Kerala in southwest India, with seafood and vegetarian dishes as specialities.

✚ H3 ✉ 6 Dering Street, W1 ☎ 020 7629 1346 🕙 Mon–Sat 12–3, 6–11 🚇 Oxford Circus, Bond Street

RHODES TWENTY FOUR £££

www.rhodes24.co.uk

Gary Rhodes provides the ultimate City experience: fine British food and amazing City views.

✚ Q4 ✉ 24th floor, Tower 42, Old Broad Street, EC2 ☎ 020 7877 7703 🕙 Mon–Fri 12–2.30, 6–9 🚇 Liverpool Street

ROYAL CHINA £–££

www.royalchinagroup.co.uk

Reserve a table or join the justifiably long lines for the best dim sum in town, served from 12–4.45.

✚ A5 ✉ 13 Queensway, W2 ☎ 020 7221 2535 🕙 Mon–Thu 12–11, Fri–Sat 12–11.30, Sun 11–10 🚇 Queensway

RULES ££

www.rules.co.uk

Rules, founded in 1798, serves good traditional English dishes in plush Edwardian rooms.

✚ K5 ✉ 35 Maiden Lane, WC2 ☎ 020 7836 5314 🕙 Mon–Sat 12–11.45, Sun 12–10.45 🚇 Covent Garden

ST. JOHN ££

www.stjohngroup.uk.com

The robust dishes on offer range from rabbit to oxtail to serious puddings, such as lemon posset.

➕ N3 ✉ 26 St. John Street, EC1 ☎ 020 3301 8069 🕐 Mon–Fri 12–3, Mon–Sat 6pm–11pm, Sun 1–3 🚇 Farringdon

THE SQUARE £££

www.squarerestaurant.com

Impressive modern French food from Philip Howard is matched by a chic but formal Mayfair interior.

➕ G5 ✉ 6–10 Bruton Street, W1 ☎ 020 7495 7100 🕐 Mon–Sat 12–2.45, 6.30–10 (10.30 Fri–Sat), Sun 6.30–9.30 🚇 Bond Street

TAMARIND ££

www.tamarindrestaurant.com

Focusing on traditional Mughal cuisine, cooked in tandoor ovens and delicately spiced, Alfred Prassad won the UK's first Michelin star for an Indian restaurant.

➕ G6 ✉ 20 Queen Street, W1 ☎ 020 7629 3561 🕐 Mon–Fri 12–2.45, 5.30–11, Sat 5.30–11, Sun 12–2.45, 6–10.30 🚇 Green Park

TATE MODERN CAFÉ £

www.tate.org.uk

Take a break from the art to enjoy upscale café food and Thames views. For a grander meal, book at the rooftop restaurant.

➕ N6 ✉ Tate Modern, SE1 ☎ 020 7401 5014 🕐 Mon–Thu 10–5.30, Fri 10–8.30, Sat 9–6.30, Sun 9–5.30 🚇 Blackfriars, Southwark

TOM AIKENS £££

www.tomaikens.co.uk

Enjoy delicious haute cuisine and superb service in a fresh, contemporary setting.

➕ D9 ✉ 43 Elystan Street, SW3 ☎ 020 7584 2003 🕐 Tue–Fri 12–2.30, 6.30–10.30, Sat 6.30–10.30 🚇 South Kensington

VILLANDRY ££

www.villandry.com

Villandry delights with its simple but tasty specialities. There's a French delicatessen, bakery, café and bar, too.

➕ G3 ✉ 170 Great Portland Street, W1 ☎ 020 7631 3131 🕐 Mon–Fri 7.30am–10.30pm, Sat 8am–10.30pm, Sun 9–6 🚇 Great Portland Street, Regents Park

WILD FOOD CAFÉ £

www.wildfoodcafe.com

Dedicated to food that makes you feel great, with creative raw and plant-based dishes (wholefood, vegan and vegetarian).

➕ K4 ✉ 1st floor, 14 Neal's Yard, WC2 ☎ 020 7419 2014 🕐 Sun–Wed 12–5, Thu–Sat 12–9.30 🚇 Covent Garden

WILD HONEY ££–£££

www.wildhoneyrestaurant.co.uk

Enjoy quality modern European cooking in a stylishly simple Mayfair setting. The set lunch and pre-theatre menus are particularly good value.

➕ G5 ✉ 12 St. George Street, W1 ☎ 020 7758 9160 🕐 Mon–Sat 12–2.30, 6–11 🚇 Oxford Circus, Bond Street

THE WOLSELEY ££

www.thewolseley.com

The Grand Café tradition continues at the Wolseley in Piccadilly. Start the day in art deco grandeur, or relax over afternoon tea after visiting the Royal Academy.

➕ H6 ✉ 160 Piccadilly, W1 ☎ 020 7499 6996 🕐 Mon–Fri 7am–midnight, Sat 8am–midnight, Sun 8am–11pm 🚇 Green Park, Piccadilly Circus

EAT

Sleep

Ranging from luxurious and modern upmarket hotels to simple budget hotels, London has accommodation to suit everyone. In this section establishments are listed alphabetically.

SLEEP

Introduction

London has many excellent hotels but room rates are very high, and it is certainly worth searching for special offers. Weekend and winter rates are often less expensive.

Reservations

Many hotels will ask you to pre-pay your reservation, or confirm with a credit card, and will charge a fee if you cancel at short notice or fail to turn up. Most hotels have rooms of different sizes, so always ask if there is a choice. Small hotels and guesthouses in historic buildings may not have a lift (elevator).

Outside Central London

If you are prepared to take a slightly longer bus or Tube ride to reach the sights, staying in a residential suburb provides a less expensive alternative to a pricey city-centre hotel.

Budget Accommodation

Consider alternatives to hotels, such as renting an apartment, staying in a bed-and-breakfast (B&B) or staying with a London family (for online information visit www.bedandbreakfast. com, www.athomeinlondon.co.uk, www. thebedandbreakfastclub.co.uk or the tourist board's Visit London website). During student vacations, inexpensive accommodation is offered by London university halls of residence (see www.universityrooms.co.uk and www.ish. org.uk). Youth hostels are another option (www.yha.org.uk).

NOISE LEVELS

As most of London's accommodation options are situated on busy streets, noise can be a problem. Some hotels have double glazing, but that can make rooms unbearably stuffy, especially since air-conditioning is not standard. If you value peace and quiet, look for hotels on side streets in residential areas; or request a room at the rear of or higher up in the building.

Top to bottom: The exclusive Claridge's Hotel; the grand entrance to The Dorchester; London's top hotels offer superb service; a room at the Grosvenor Hotel

SLEEP

Directory

South Bank
Budget
Premier Inn
Mid-Range
Southwark Rose

Fleet Street to the Tower
Budget
Travelodge
Mid-Range
Chamberlain
Zetter Rooms
Luxury
Andaz
Malmaison
The Rookery

Covent Garden to Regent's Park
Budget
Generator Hostel
Morgan
Mid-Range
Academy
Luxury
Charlotte Street Hotel
Covent Garden Hotel
Hazlitt's
One Aldwych

St. Martin's Lane
Savoy

Westminster and St. James's
Luxury
The Goring
The Ritz

Around Hyde Park
Budget
22 York Street
Easyhotel
Pavilion Hotel
Mid-Range
Aster House
Kensington House
The Leonard
Luxury
The Berkeley
Blakes
The Dorchester
The Halkin

Further Afield
Budget
Clink 261
Mid-Range
Portobello

Sleeping A–Z

PRICES

Prices are approximate and based on a double room for one night.

£££	Over £250
££	£150–£250
£	under £150

22 YORK STREET £
www.22yorkstreet.co.uk
This elegant five-storey Georgian town house close to Regent's Park has been transformed into a quality bed-and-breakfast.
🚇 E3 ✉ 22 York Street, W1 ☎ 020 7224 2990 🚇 Baker Street

ACADEMY ££
www.theetoncollection.co.uk
Convenient for the British Museum, this 49-room boutique hotel is set in five converted Georgian town houses.
🚇 J3 ✉ 21 Gower Street, WC1 ☎ 020 7631 4115 🚇 Goodge Street

ANDAZ £££

www.london.liverpoolstreet.andaz.hyatt.com
Casual 21st-century luxury is the theme of this stylishly converted Victorian railway hotel.
➕ R3 ✉ 40 Liverpool Street, EC2 ☎ 020 7961 1234 🚇 Liverpool Street

ASTER HOUSE ££

www.asterhouse.com
Aster House stands with other chic B&Bs in a smart South Kensington stuccoed terrace, near the museums. You can enjoy the garden, palm-filled conservatory and power showers.
➕ C9 ✉ 3 Sumner Place, SW7 ☎ 020 7581 5888 🚇 South Kensington

THE BERKELEY £££

www.the-berkeley.co.uk
Guests at this luxury Knightsbridge hotel enjoy traditional elegance, plus famed service and food. Facilities include a spa, rooftop pool and two great restaurants.
➕ E7 ✉ Wilton Place, SW1 ☎ 020 7235 6000 🚇 Hyde Park Corner, Knightsbridge

BLAKES ££–£££

www.blakeshotels.com
Designer Anoushka Hempel has achieved sumptuous decadence in this South Kensington boutique

LOCATION

It is well worth perusing the London map to decide where you are likely to spend most of your time. Then select a hotel in that area or accessible to it by Underground on a direct line, so you avoid having to change trains. London is vast and it takes time to cross, particularly by bus and costly taxis. By paying a little more to be in the heart of the city, you will save on travel time and costs.

hotel. There are just 41 rooms, plus a restaurant and bar.
➕ Off map ✉ 33 Roland Gardens, SW7 ☎ 020 7370 6701 🚇 South Kensington, Gloucester Road

CHAMBERLAIN ££

www.fullershotels.com
In lavishly converted 20th-century offices in the City of London, this hotel has 64 comfortable bedrooms. There is a popular pub on the premises.
➕ S4 ✉ 130–135 Minories, EC3 ☎ 020 7680 1500 🚇 Fenchurch Street, Aldgate

CHARLOTTE STREET HOTEL £££

www.firmdalehotels.com
Kit and Tim Kemp's boutique cocktail of comfort and fairy-tale Englishness has 52 rooms.
➕ H3 ✉ 15 Charlotte Street, W1 ☎ 020 7806 2000 🚇 Goodge Street

CLINK 261 £

www.clinkhostels.com
This funky backpacker hostel, convenient for Eurostar departures from London St. Pancras, has 170 beds in 33 rooms.
➕ K1 ✉ 261–265 Gray's Inn Road, WC1 ☎ 020 7713 7789 🚇 King's Cross

COVENT GARDEN HOTEL £££

www.firmdalehotels.com
Another of Kit Kemp's stylish boutique hotels, this one attracts film stars who enjoy its 58 traditional yet contemporary British rooms, bathrooms and library.
➕ J4 ✉ 10 Monmouth Street, WC2 ☎ 020 7806 1000 🚇 Leicester Square

THE DORCHESTER £££

www.thedorchester.com
The Dorchester is one of London's finest hotels. Deliciously art deco,

it is a London landmark from its grand entrance and piano bar to the Oliver Messel suite. The hotel's some 250 bedrooms have huge, luxury bathrooms.

➕ F6 ✉ Park Lane, W1 ☎ 020 7629 8888 🚇 Green Park, Hyde Park Corner

EASYHOTEL £

www.easyhotel.com
Easyhotel is inexpensive but basic in the extreme; few of the 34 rooms have windows.

➕ A8 ✉ 14 Lexham Gardens, W8 ☎ Reserve by website only 🚇 Earl's Court, Gloucester Road

GENERATOR HOSTEL £

www.generatorhostels.com
This industrial-style building has 217 rooms, and offers 870 guests bunk-bedded rooms, excellent facilities and a party atmosphere.

➕ K2 ✉ 37 Tavistock Place, WC1 ☎ 020 7388 7666 🚇 Russell Square

THE GORING £££

www.thegoring.com
High standards of old-fashioned hospitality and service make this

splendid hotel, with 74 classic rooms, memorable. It's where the Middleton family stayed before Kate's wedding to Prince William.

➕ G8 ✉ Beeston Place, Grosvenor Gardens, SW1 ☎ 020 7396 9000 🚇 Victoria

THE HALKIN £££

www.comohotels.com/thehalkin
Opened 20 years ago, central London's first boutique hotel blends Western and Asian aesthetics. It has 41 rooms and a good Basque restaurant.

➕ F7 ✉ 4 Halkin Street, SW1 ☎ 020 7333 1059 🚇 Hyde Park Corner

SLEEP

The Dorchester, one of the capital's finest hotels

London has many contemporary hotels, from starkly minimal to sumptuously luxurious. At the top end, try the Andaz Hotel (▷ 156), Kit Kemp's six London hotels (www.firmdalehotels.com), Schrager's Sanderson (✉ 50 Berners Street, W1 ☎ 020 7300 1400; www.sandersonlondon.com), No. 5 Maddox Street (✉ 5 Maddox Street, W1 ☎ 020 7647 0200; www.living-rooms.co.uk) or myhotel Bloomsbury (✉ 11–13 Bayley Street, Bedford Square, WC1 ☎ 020 3004 6000; www.myhotels.co.uk) near the British Museum.

The Savoy, a byword for luxury

SLEEP

HAZLITT'S £££
www.hazlittshotel.com
The 23-room Hazlitt's has near-perfect period decoration in three 18th-century houses, plus it's in a superb location for theatreland.
➕ J4 ✉ 6 Frith Street, W1 ☎ 020 7434 1771 🚇 Tottenham Court Road

KENSINGTON HOUSE ££
www.kenhouse.com
This beautifully restored 19th-century property provides contemporary accommodation in the heart of Kensington. The 41 bedrooms are light and stylish.
➕ A7 ✉ 15–16 Prince of Wales Terrace, W8 ☎ 020 7937 2345 🚇 High Street Kensington

THE LEONARD ££–£££
www.theleonard.com
A discreet, small hotel, near busy Oxford Street, the Leonard has 28 comfortable bedrooms and luxury apartments.
➕ E4 ✉ 15 Seymour Street, W1 ☎ 020 7935 2010 🚇 Marble Arch

MALMAISON £££
www.malmaison.com
Relax in the stylish, contemporary rooms at this hotel with a brasserie and bar in trendy Clerkenwell.
➕ N3 ✉ 18 Charterhouse Square, EC1 ☎ 0844 693 0656 🚇 Farringdon

MORGAN £
www.morganhotel.co.uk
Family-run, friendly and well-located, the Morgan has just 20 rooms, so book ahead.
➕ J3 ✉ 24 Bloomsbury Street, WC1 ☎ 020 7636 3735 🚇 Tottenham Court Road

ONE ALDWYCH £££
www.onealdwych.com
A stylish, 105-room contemporary hotel in an Edwardian building, One Aldwych epitomizes restrained luxury.
➕ L5 ✉ 1 Aldwych, WC2 ☎ 020 7300 1000 🚇 Covent Garden, Temple

PAVILION HOTEL £
www.pavilionhoteluk.com
The plain facade at the 30-room Pavilion Hotel belies the witty fantasy decor inside.
➕ C4 ✉ 34–36 Sussex Gardens, W2 ☎ 020 7262 0905 🚇 Paddington

PORTOBELLO ££
www.portobello-hotel.co.uk
A romantic retreat with 24 exotic, sumptuous rooms, the hotel is

within easy reach of the antiques shops of Portobello Road.

✛ Off map ✉ 22 Stanley Gardens, W11 ☎ 020 7727 2777 Ⓩ Notting Hill Gate

PREMIER INN £

www.premierinn.com

In County Hall, opposite the Houses of Parliament, this 313-room hotel is the star London location of the no-frills chain.

✛ L7 ✉ County Hall, Belvedere Road, SE1 ☎ 0871 527 8648 Ⓩ Waterloo

THE RITZ £££

www.theritzlondon.com

Guests enjoy sumptuous luxury, with traditional style, gilt decor and the great first-floor promenade to London's most beautiful dining room, overlooking Green Park.

✛ G6 ✉ 150 Piccadilly, W1 ☎ 020 7493 8181 Ⓩ Green Park

THE ROOKERY £££

www.rookeryhotel.co.uk

Enjoy discreet comforts in this atmospheric 33-room hotel, enhanced with antiques, open fires and Victorian bathrooms.

✛ N3 ✉ Cowcross Street, EC1 ☎ 020 7336 0931 Ⓩ Farringdon

ST. MARTIN'S LANE £££

www.stmartinslane.com

Ian Schrager and Philippe Starck's fabulous 204-room hotel in Covent Garden is a celebration of theatrical minimalism.

✛ J5 ✉ 45 St. Martin's Lane, WC2 ☎ 020 7300 5500 Ⓩ Covent Garden, Leicester Square

SAVOY £££

www.fairmont.com/savoy-london

A top-to-toe refurbishment has brought this grand London hotel

firmly into the 21st century. It has a perfect spot next to the Thames.

✛ L5 ✉ Strand, WC2 ☎ 020 7836 4343 Ⓩ Covent Garden

SOUTHWARK ROSE £–££

www.ibis.com

This Ibis Styles hotel with 114 rooms is close to Tate Modern and, via the Millennium Bridge, the rest of the city centre. ✛ P6 ✉ 43–47 Southwark Bridge Road, SE1 ☎ 020 7015 1480 Ⓩ London Bridge

TRAVELODGE £

www.travelodge.co.uk

Part of the no-frills chain, this central Travelodge is a good budget choice.

✛ S5 ✉ 1 Goodmans Yard, Lloyds Court Business Centre, E1 ☎ 0871 984 6388 Ⓩ Tower Hill

ZETTER ROOMS ££

www.thezetter.com

A hip contemporary hotel in Clerkenwell, with a restaurant and bar to match, the Zetter has 59 rooms. There are great views of the City from the rooftop suites.

✛ N2 ✉ St. John's Square, 86–88 Clerkenwell Road, EC1 ☎ 020 7324 4444 Ⓩ Farringdon

SLEEP

BARGAIN LUXURY

To be pampered amid sumptuous surroundings may be an essential part of your trip. London's most luxurious hotels have been built with no expense spared. Hotel prices are generally very high, but quality rooms can be had for bargain prices. It's always worth asking when you make your reservation whether any special deals are available. Most deluxe and mid-range hotels offer weekend deals throughout the year.

Need to Know

This section takes you through all the practical aspects of your trip to make it run more smoothly and to give you confidence before you go and while you are there.

NEED TO KNOW

Planning Ahead

WHEN TO GO

The tourist season is year-round, and most attractions remain open all year. Peak season is from June to September, when you should arrive with a hotel reservation and theatre tickets. The quietest months are February, March, October and November, when hotels may give a discount.

TIME

GMT (Greenwich Mean Time) is standard. BST (British Summer Time) is 1 hour ahead (late Mar–late Oct).

TEMPERATURE

JAN	FEB	MAR	APR	MAY	JUN	JUL	AUG	SEP	OCT	NOV	DEC
42°F	45°F	50°F	55°F	63°F	68°F	72°F	72°F	66°F	57°F	50°F	45°F
6°C	7°C	10°C	13°C	17°C	20°C	22°C	22°C	19°C	14°C	10°C	7°C

Spring (March to May) has a mixture of sunshine and showers, although winter often encroaches on it.

Summer (June to August) can be unpredictable, with clear skies and hot days interspersed with rain, sultry greyness or thunderstorms.

Autumn (September to November) has clear skies that can feel almost summery. Real autumn starts in October, and colder weather sets in during November.

Winter (December to February) is generally fairly cold, and snow has been disruptive in recent years.

WHAT'S ON

January *Sales:* Shopping bargains at stores all over the city.

February *Chinese New Year:* Dragon dances and fireworks in Chinatown.

March *Chelsea Antiques Fair:* Chelsea Old Town Hall.

April *Oxford and Cambridge Boat Race* (1st Sat): This famous annual race takes place on the Thames from Putney to Mortlake.

London Marathon: The world's biggest running race.

May *Chelsea Flower Show* (end of May): One of the world's best shows takes place at the Royal Hospital, Chelsea.

June *Trooping the Colour* (2nd Sat): The 'Colours' (flags) are trooped before the Queen on Horseguards Parade, Whitehall.

Wimbledon (Jun/Jul): The world's leading grass tennis tournament.

July *Promenade Concerts* (Jul–Aug): Nightly world-class classical concerts in the Albert Hall.

August *Notting Hill Carnival* (last Sun and Bank Holiday Monday): Europe's biggest carnival.

September *Mayor's Thames Festival:* London's largest outdoor arts festival, a free weekend extravaganza on and around the river.

October *The Big Draw:* The world's largest celebration of drawing.

BFI London Film Festival.

November *Bonfire Night* (5 Nov): Fires and fireworks commemorate the failed Gunpowder Plot of 1605.

Lord Mayor's Show: The City of London's favourite ritual, with parades and pageantry in a long procession.

December *Christmas music* (all month): Christmas music fills London's churches.

USEFUL WEBSITES

www.visitlondon.com
London's official site is up-to-date and comprehensive with ideas for museums, theatre and restaurants, and sections for children and visitors with disabilities. It offers discounts, too.

www.royalparks.org.uk
From Greenwich Park to Green Park, all eight of London's Royal Parks are detailed here, with information on special events and activities for children.

www.tfl.gov.uk
London Transport's official site gives ideas for what to see and do, ticket information for the Underground, buses, DLR and river services. It also has a WAP-enabled journey planner.

www.royal.gov.uk
The official site of the British royal family, with history, royal residences, who's doing what today and a monthly online magazine.

www.bhrconline.com
The British Hotel Reservation Centre website takes bookings, from bed-and-breakfasts to grand hotels. Special discounts are included.

www.londontown.com
This comprehensive site covers what's on, what's new, attractions, events, theatres, sightseeing ideas, traditions, nightlife, shopping, markets and general advice.

www.hrp.org.uk
This site is dedicated to London's five great historic palaces, from the Tower of London to Hampton Court Palace.

www.officiallondontheatre.co.uk
The Society of London Theatre's official site, with all the latest theatre news, together with comprehensive interviews with stars, performance details and theatre access for visitors with disabilities.

PRIME TRAVEL SITES

www.nationaltrust.org.uk
This independent organization owns and maintains many buildings and extensive lands, some of them in and around London.

www.english-heritage.org.uk/London
English Heritage is responsible for many historic sites and buildings—with ideas for days out in London.

www.fodors.com
A complete travel-planning site. You can research prices and weather; book air tickets, cars and rooms; pose questions (and get answers) from fellow travellers; and find links to other sites.

www.visitbritain.com
Great places to visit around the UK, with accommodation, transport, special offers and travel tips.

INTERNET CAFÉS

● All of the capital's public libraries have internet facilities. WiFi is available at Starbucks cafés, major train stations and airports. Most hotels have modem plug-in-points (data ports) or WiFi in each room.

Getting There

Savvy Londoners use the
Heathrow Connect service
(www.heathrowconnect.com)
to Paddington station. Two
trains an hour operate on
this stopping service; the
journey time is around 25
minutes and the cost is less
than half of the express fares.

TRAINS

● For all information
☎ 08457 484950;
www.nationalrail.co.uk
● Purchase tickets at the
railway station or on online
at www.thetrainline.com.
● All major London train
stations are on Tube lines.
● There are eight major
London train stations; sometimes a town is served by
more than one (e.g.,
Paddington and Waterloo
both serve Windsor).
● Train fares are high but
there are lots of cheap deals
if you book in advance and
can be flexible about the time
you travel.

AIRPORTS

Heathrow and Gatwick are the principal airports serving
the city. However, Stansted, Luton and London City are
becoming increasingly busy with traffic from Continental
Europe. There are train links to the continent via Lille
and Paris and road links to Channel ports.

60km (40 miles)

Luton Airport 🗙
Bus 1hr 30 min
Train 25 min

🗙 **Stansted Airport**
Bus 1hr 40 min
Train 40 min

🗙 **London City Airport**
Bus 25–40 min
DLR/Underground 25 min

Heathrow Airport 🗙
Bus approx 1hr
Train approx 15 min
Underground 1hr

🗙 **Gatwick Airport**
Bus 1hr 30 min–2hr 45 min
Train 30 min

FROM HEATHROW

Heathrow (tel 0834 335 1801; www.
heathrowairport.com) has five terminals,
32km (20 miles) west of central London; all
are well served by public transport. The Tube's
Piccadilly line runs from 5am to 11.40pm
(Heathrow Terminal 4 station closes Mon–Sat
11.35pm, Sun 11.15pm); and takes about an
hour. The Heathrow Express (tel 0845 600
1515; www.heathrowexpress. com), a high-
speed rail link to Paddington station, runs
from 5.10am to 11.40pm every 15 minutes.
Prices are high for the 15-minute journey.
National Express (tel 08717 818181; www.
nationalexpress.com) buses run from 5.30am
to 9pm to Victoria Coach Station, journey
time around one hour. Taxis wait outside the
terminals; the trip takes under an hour,
depending on traffic, and costs around £70
(www.heathrowtaxis.org).

FROM GATWICK

Gatwick airport (tel 0844 892 0322; www.
gatwickairport.com) is 48km (30 miles) south
of the heart of the city. The best way to reach
London is by train. The Gatwick Express
(tel 0845 850 1530; www.gatwickexpress.

com) train leaves for Victoria Station every 15 minutes, (4.35am–12.50am) and takes 30 minutes. Southern runs slightly slower but cheaper services; and First Capital Connect's Thameslink leads direct to the City and King's Cross/St. Pancras International. Taxis cost more than £100.

FROM STANSTED

Stansted airport (tel 0844 335 1803; www. stanstedairport.com) is 56km (35 miles) northeast of central London. The Stansted Express (tel 0845 850 0150; www. stanstedexpress.com) to Liverpool Street Station takes around 50 minutes. Several bus/coach operators run services to Liverpool Street and Victoria stations. Journey time is up to 1 hour 40 minutes. A taxi costs from £100.

FROM LUTON AIRPORT

Luton airport (tel 01582 405 100; www.london-luton.co.uk) is 53km (33 miles) north of London. There are bus links to Victoria Coach Station, taking around 1 hour 30 minutes, and East Midlands and Thameslink trains to St. Pancras International, taking from 25 minutes. Taxis cost about £80.

FROM LONDON CITY AIRPORT

City Airport (tel 020 7646 0088; www.londoncityairport.com) is at Royal Albert Docks, 14km (9 miles) east of central London. Trains from London City Airport DLR station feed into the Underground system. Taxis from the terminal cost around £35.

THE CHANNEL TUNNEL

Eurostar train services (tel 08432 186186; www.eurostar.com) connect Britain to Continental Europe, and are a great way of arriving in London, plus taking trips out to Paris, Brussels and elsewhere. Book ahead for cheap deals. Trains use St. Pancras International terminal, close to King's Cross. Eurotunnel (tel 08433 353535; www.eurotunnel.com) is for vehicles only. Fares are lower if you reserve ahead.

If you travel to London by long-distance coach you will probably arrive at Victoria Coach Station (VCS) on Buckingham Palace Road, near Victoria main train station. The coach station is a few minutes' walk from the Underground station, which is on the Victoria, District and Circle lines. Alternatively, there is a taxi rank immediately outside VCS.

The most seasoned traveller occasionally leaves something behind—airlines find forgotten computers almost daily.

● Contact the place where you think you left it or saw it last.

● Report the loss to a police station and get a copy of the report form for your insurance claim.

● If you lose your passport, report it to the police and your embassy. Provided you have photocopies of the key pages, it should not be difficult to replace but there's usually a charge.

● Contact for London Transport and taxi lost property ☎ 0343 222 1234; www.tfl.gov.uk.

Getting Around

DRIVING TIP

Driving in London is slow, parking is expensive and fines are high. Congestion charges operate from Monday to Friday, 7am–6pm, costing £10 a day. Do not drive in London unless you have to: use public transport.

VISITORS WITH DISABILITIES

London is steadily improving its facilities for visitors with disabilities, from shops and theatres to hotels and museums. The Government is introducing free admission for those with disabilities. Newer attractions such as Tate Modern and the London Eye are better equipped than ancient buildings such as Westminster Abbey. Check out the London Tourist Board's comprehensive website (www.visitlondon.com) and guide books, such as *Access in London* (published by Access Project PHSP ✉ 39 Bradley Gardens, W13; www.accessinlondon.org). Also consult Artsline (www.artsline.org.uk), Can Be Done (www.canbedone.co.uk) and Dial (www.scope.org.uk/dial). William Forrester, a lecturer and wheelchair user, leads tailor-made tours in the city (☎ 01483 575401).

Underground trains (known as the Tube) and buses run from around 5.30am to just after midnight, when service is via a night bus. The transport system is divided into zones (clearly indicated on transport maps) and you must have a ticket valid for the zone you are in. If you anticipate making more than one journey, buy a Travelcard (▷ 167), which allows unlimited use of the Underground, buses and Docklands Light Railway (DLR) services. Travel information is available on tel 0343 222 1234; www.tfl.gov.uk.

THE UNDERGROUND (TUBE)

Twelve colour-coded lines link almost 300 stations. Use a travel pass or buy a ticket from a machine or ticket booth; keep the ticket until the end of the journey. The system includes the Docklands Light Railway (DLR).

BUSES

Plan your journey using the latest copy of the Central London bus guide available at London Transport information centres (▷ 167) or at www.tfl.gov.uk. A flat cash fare applies across London. Tickets must be bought from a machine at the bus stop. A bus stop is indicated by a red sign on a metal pole displaying diagrams of each route it serves.

Look out for the new red double-decker buses, combining cutting-edge design and technology with nostalgia for the old Routemaster buses.

TAXIS

Taxis that are available for rental illuminate a yellow 'For Hire' sign on the roof. Hold out your hand to hail them beside the road. Drivers of official cabs will know the city well. They are obliged to follow the shortest route unless an alternative is agreed beforehand. A 'black cab' (now often not black but a bright colour) is licensed for up to five passengers. Meter charges increase in the evenings and at weekends. Avoid minicabs if you can as they may have no meter and possibly inadequate insurance. Call a black cab via Radio Taxis (tel 020 7272 0272; www.radiotaxis.co.uk).

TRAVEL INFORMATION CENTRES

These sell travel passes and provide Tube and train maps, bus route maps and information on cheap tickets. They are open daily at the following stations: Heathrow terminals 1, 2 and 3, Liverpool Street, Victoria, Euston, King's Cross and Piccadilly Circus. Transport for London service, tel 0343 222 1234.

TRAVEL PASSES

Travelcards, valid after 9.30am (you must pay a surcharge to use them earlier), for unlimited travel by Tube, railway, Docklands Light Railway and buses, are sold at travel information centres, railway and Tube stations, and some shops. They cover travel for one day or seven days.

Oyster prepay Smartcards are valid for use on the Underground, DLR, bus, Thameslink and some national rail networks. Single fares are much cheaper with Oyster than cash and the cards can be topped up with more credit.

LONDON PASS

This is a pass to more than 50 top attractions as well as an option to travel on buses, the Tube and trains. The aim of the pass is to enable you to beat the crowds lining up at selected major attractions. The pass is valid for either one, two, three or six days—multi-day passes must be used on consecutive days. It offers discounts on restaurants and leisure activities. See www.londonpass.com for details.

BOATING AND BIKING

Thames Clippers (www.thamesclippers.com) runs a commuter, leisure and sightseeing service aboard high-speed catamarans.

London Cycling Campaign (www.lcc.org.uk) can advise on all aspects of biking in the capital. Visitors can rent a bicycle from one of the hundreds of Barclays Cycle Hire project docking stations scattered across London (www.tfl. gov.uk).

● By water (▷ 56–57).

TIPS

● London is huge. It may take more than an hour to reach your destination, so allow plenty of time—and plan your day to avoid criss-crossing the city.
● Buy a travelcard, which is valid for the entire transport network. Select the appropriate pass for the areas you will visit. Many people find the Zones 1 and 2 range is adequate; pay a supplement when you go outside it.
● Use common sense when travelling alone at night, but there is no need to be unduly concerned.
● Smoking is banned on all public transport.

FUN TOURS

There are many quirky ways to see London. Below are some ideas:
● London Walks (☎ 020 7624 3978; www.walks.com).
● Open House Architecture (☎ 020 3006 7008; www.open-city.org.uk).
● By water (▷ 56–57).
● London Duck Tours (☎ 020 7928 3132; www.londonducktours.co.uk).
● Cable car (☎ 0343 222 1234; www.emiratesairline. co.uk). London's newest transport link is the Emirates Air Line. A cable car across the Thames between North Greenwich and the Royal Docks, it offers easy access to the O2 Arena with great views along the way.

Essential Facts

VISAS AND TRAVEL INSURANCE

Check visa and passport requirements before travelling, see www.fco.gov.uk or ukinusa.fco.gov.uk. EU citizens are covered for medical expenses with an EHIC card; insurance to cover illness and theft is still strongly advised. Visitors from outside the EU should check their insurance coverage and if necessary, buy a supplementary policy.

MONEY

Try to arrive at the airport or train station with some British coins or some £10 or £5 notes. If you travel to your hotel by Tube, the self-service machines accept both money and credit cards.

CREDIT CARDS

● Credit cards are widely accepted; Visa and MasterCard are the most popular, followed by AmericanExpress, Diners Club and JCB. Credit cards can also be used for withdrawing cash from ATMs at any bank displaying the appropriate sign.

● If your credit cards are lost, report each one immediately to the relevant company and the police; also call your bank. To discover your credit card company's local 24-hour emergency number, go to www.ukphonebook.com; it's free but you have to register.

ELECTRICITY

● Standard supply is 240V. Motor-driven equipment needs a specific frequency; in the UK it is 50 cycles per second (kHz).

EMERGENCY TELEPHONE NUMBERS

● For police, fire or ambulance, tel 999 from any telephone, free of charge. The call goes directly to the emergency services. Tell the operator which street you are on and the nearest landmark, intersection or house number; stay by the telephone until help arrives.

MEDICAL TREATMENT

● EU nationals and citizens of some other countries with special arrangements (Australia and New Zealand) may be eligible to receive free National Health Service (NHS) medical treatment provided that they are in possession of the correct documentation (an EHIC card for EU visitors).

● All other visitors have to pay.

● If you need an ambulance tel 999 on any telephone, free of charge, or 112 from most mobiles/cellphones.

● NHS hospitals with 24-hour emergency departments include: University College Hospital, Gower Street (entrance in Grafton Way), WC1, tel 020 3456 7890; St Mary's Hospital, South Wharf Road, W2, tel 020 3312 6330.

● Private hospitals, with no emergency unit, include the Cromwell Hospital, 162–174 Cromwell Road, SW5, tel 020 7460 2000.

● NHS Direct: tel 111; www.nhsdirect.nhs.uk.

● Dental problems: King's College Hospital, Denmark Hill, SE5, has an Acute Dental Care clinic for treating serious dental problems. Helpdesk tel 020 3299 3052; Mon–Fri 9–4.30.

● Eye specialist: Moorfields Eye Hospital, City Road, EC1, tel 020 7253 3411; Vision Express, 263–265 Oxford Street, W1, tel 020 7409 7880 (includes an opticians and an on-site workshop for glasses and contact lenses).

● For homeopathic pharmacies, practitioners and advice, contact the British Homeopathic Association, tel 01582 408675; www.britishhomeopathic.org.

MEDICINES
● Many drugs cannot be bought over the counter. For an NHS prescription, you pay a modest flat rate; if a private doctor prescribes, you pay the full cost. To claim charges back on insurance, keep receipts.
● Chemists that keep longer hours include: Bliss Chemist, 5 Marble Arch, W1, tel 020 7723 6116, daily 9am–midnight; Boots Midnight Pharmacy, 44–6 Regent Street, Piccadilly Circus, W1, tel 020 7734 6126, Mon–Fri 8am–midnight, Sat 9am–midnight, Sun 12–6.30.

OPENING HOURS
● Major attractions: seven days a week; some open late certain days of each week.
● Shops: generally Mon–Sat 9.30/10am–6pm; department stores until 8 or even 10pm (Selfridges, Oxford Street). Many shops open Sun 12–5/6pm; department stores have 'browsing time' before the tills open from 11.30am. Late-night shopping (until 8pm) is on Thu in the West End and Wed in Knightsbridge.
● Banks: Mon–Fri 9.30–5; a few remain open later or open on Sat mornings. *Bureaux de change* generally have longer opening hours. ATMs are abundant.
● Post offices: usually Mon–Fri 9–5.30, Sat 9–12.30.

NEWSPAPERS AND MAGAZINES
Newspapers include the *Financial Times*, *The Daily Telegraph*, *The Independent*, *The Guardian*, *The Daily Mail* and *The Times*, Sunday papers include *The Sunday Times*, *Sunday Telegraph*, *The Observer* and *Independent on Sunday*. Free papers (Mon–Fri) are *Metro* and *London Evening Standard*, which is strong on entertainment and nightlife (www.thisislondon.co.uk). *Time Out* (www.timeout. com), published weekly on Wed), lists almost everything going and is free.

TIPPING
Many restaurants add a 12.5 per cent service charge. For taxis, hairdressers and other services, 10 per cent is acceptable. Tips are not usual in theatres, cinemas or concert halls, or in pubs or bars (unless there is table service).

EMBASSIES

Australian High Commission	✉ Australia House, Strand, WC2 ☎ 020 7379 4334; www.uk.embassy.gov.au
Canadian High Commission	✉ 1 Grosvenor Square, W1 ☎ 020 7258 6600; www.canadainternational.gc.ca
New Zealand High Commission	✉ New Zealand House, 80 Haymarket, SW1 ☎ 020 7930 8422; www.nzembassy.com
Embassy of the US	✉ 24 Grosvenor Square, W1 ☎ 020 7499 9000; http://london.usembassy.gov

MAILING A LETTER

Stamps are sold at post offices and some newsagents and shops. Trafalgar Square Post Office stays open late:
✉ William IV Street, WC2
🕐 Mon–Fri 8.30–6.30, Sat 9–5.30. Letter boxes are red.

TELEVISION

● Excluding satellite, cable and digital, there are five main national terrestrial channels in Britain: BBC1, BBC2, ITV1, Channel 4 and Channel 5. The BBC is funded by a licence fee and there is no advertising on any BBC channels.

● Relatively few homes in Britain have cable, although it is increasing. Digital terrestrial and digital satellite television services can be received in all homes, with a large number of channels and wide variety of content, available either free or through subscription. Programmes can also be viewed on the internet and 3G mobile/cell phones.

STUDENTS

Holders of an International Student Identity Card will be able to obtain some good concessions on travel and entrance fees.

PUBLIC HOLIDAYS

● 1 Jan; Good Fri; Easter Mon; May Day (first Mon in May); last Mon in May; last Mon in Aug; 25 Dec; 26 Dec.

● Almost all attractions and shops close Christmas Day; many close 24 Dec, 1 Jan and Good Fri as well. Some shops, restaurants and attractions remain open throughout, but check.

SENSIBLE PRECAUTIONS

● Keep valuables in a hotel or bank safe box.

● Note all passport, ticket and credit card numbers, and keep separately. Carry photocopies of the key pages of your passport.

● Make sure that bags are fully closed and keep them in sight at all times—do not put them on the floor or over the back of a chair.

● At night, try not to travel alone; if you must, either prebook a taxi (not a mini-cab) or keep to well-lit streets and use a bus or Tube train where there are other people.

PHONES

● London numbers (now 8 digits) are prefixed with the code 020 when dialling from outside the city. To call London from abroad, dial the country code 44, then just 20, then the 8 digit number.

● Public phones accept coins, phonecards and credit cards.

● For the operator tel 100. For the international operator or to reverse charges tel 155.

● Directory enquiries: there are many options; tel 0800 953 0720 for details and prices.

● To make international calls from the UK, dial 00, then the country code (1 for the US).

● Beware of high charges on numbers prefixed 08 or 09 (0800 is free, 0845 and 0843 inexpensive).

● Before departure, consult with your cell/mobile phone provider on coverage and rates.

TOURIST INFORMATION
● London Information Centre

Leicester Square, W1, tel 020 7292 2333; www.londoninformationcentre.com; daily 8am–midnight, Leicester Square.

Books and Films

London's vitality, variety, glamour and squalor have always provided rich pickings for writers and film makers.

London: The Biography (2000), *Thames: Secret River* (2007) and *London Under* (2011) by historian Peter Ackroyd are essential background reading for visitors to the city. For fans of historical fiction, C.J. Sansom's Matthew Shardlake series (2003–11) evokes London at the time of Henry VIII.

Muriel Spark used life in post-war Kensington as the setting for her novella *The Girls of Slender Means* (1963); in *A Severed Head* (1961), Iris Murdoch foresaw the sexual revolution and swinging London of the 1960s, while Doris Lessing had her character Martha Quest experience the social changes of the Cold War years in her controversial *The Four-Gated City* (1969). The amusing *Bridget Jones's Diary* (1997) by Helen Fielding defined a generation of 30-something women living in London in the late 1990s.

With his autobiographical *Fever Pitch* (1992) and fictional *About a Boy* (1998), Nick Hornby took a different angle on youthful London, as did Hanif Kureishi with his mixed-race teenage protagonist Karim in *The Buddha of Suburbia* (1990).

At the turn of the 21st century, multinational, multi-denominational London was being explored by writers such as Zadie Smith in *White Teeth* (2001), Monica Ali in *Brick Lane* (2001) and Andrea Levy, who delved into migration from the Caribbean in the excellent *Small Island* (2004).

Several of these more recent novels have made their way onto the big screen, but for many people the most iconic movies are Michael Caine's lad-about-town *Alfie* (1966), the crime comedy *A Fish Called Wanda* (1988), the two *Bridget Jones* films (2001, 2004) and writer/director Richard Curtis's romantic comedies *Four Weddings and a Funeral* (1994), *Notting Hill* (1999) and *Love Actually* (2003), with the oh-so-English Hugh Grant in their leading roles.

LONDON CLASSICS

Perhaps the most famous book about London is *The Diary of Samuel Pepys*, in which the observer, Pepys, recorded events from 1600 to 1669. Many of Charles Dickens' novels have London settings, including *Oliver Twist* (1837), *The Old Curiosity Shop* (1840), *Bleak House* (1853) and *Little Dorrit* (1857). In 1887, Sir Arthur Conan Doyle introduced his character Sherlock Holmes in the novel *A Study in Scarlet*. The legendary fictional detective lived at 221b Baker Street, W1. In William Thackeray's *Vanity Fair* (1847), Becky Sharp begins her adventures in Russell Square. Humorist P.G. Wodehouse, creator of the eccentric Jeeves and Wooster, based his Drones Club on several London gentlemen's clubs of the time (1920s).

Index

The Automobile Association would like to thank the following photographers, companies and picture libraries for their assistance in the preparation of this book.

2 top to bottom i) AA/Sarah Montgomery; ii) AA/Neil Setchfield; iii) AA/James Tims; iv) AA/Sarah Montgomery; v) AA/James Tims; **3 top to bottom** i) AA/James Tims; ii) AA/James Tims; iii) AA/Robert Mort; iv) AA/Sarah Montgomery; **4tl** AA/James Tims; **5** AA/James Tims; **6/7 clockwise from top** i) Kathy deWitt/Alamy; ii) Julio Etchart/Alamy; iii) Courtesy Arup; iv) Courtesy Transport for London; v) Julio Etchart/Alamy; vi) Julio Etchart/Alamy; **8/9 clockwise from top** i) AA/Sarah Montgomery; ii) AA/James Tims; iii) AA/James Tims; iv) AA/Neil Setchfield; v) AA/James Tims; vi) AA/Neil Setchfield; **10bl** AA/James Tims; **10br** The Art Archive/Alamy; **11bl** Mary Evans Picture Library/Alamy; **11br** AA/James Tims; **12** AA/Neil Setchfield; **14tl** AA/James Tims; **14tr** AA/Sarah Montgomery; **14cr/15c** AA/James Tims; **15tl/16t** AA/James Tims; **17tl** AA/Neil Setchfield; **17tr/17c** AA/James Tims; **18t/19tl** AA/James Tims; **19tc** AA/Sarah Montgomery; **19tr** Courtesy Royal Collection 2011, Her Majesty Queen Elizabeth II/Derry Moore; **19c** Monica Wells/TTL; **20t** AA/Neil Setchfield; **21tl** AA/AA; **21cl** AA/S and O Mathews; **21c** AA/Neil Setchfield; **22t/23tl-22c/23cl, 23c, 23 tr** AA/James Tims; **24t** London Stills; **25tl** AA/James Tims; **25tr** AA/Sarah Montgomery; **25cl** London Stills; **25cr** AA/James Tims; **26t** Courtesy Harvey Nichols; **27tl** Courtesy Swarovski/Yellow Door; **27tr** Travelshots.com/Alamy; **27cl** Courtesy Harvey Nichols; **27cr** AA/Sarah Montgomery; **28t** Courtesy EDF Energy London Eye/British Tourist Authority/James McCormick; **29tl-29tr-29c** Courtesy EDF Energy London Eye; **30t/31tl** Courtesy Museum of London; **31tr-31cr** AA/James Tims; **32t** Ronald Weir/TTL; **33tl-33cl-33c** AA/James Tims; **33tr** Courtesy The National Gallery; **34t** Courtesy The National Portrait Gallery; **35tl** Courtesy The National Portrait Gallery/Andrew Putler; **35tr-35cr** AA/James Tims; **35cl** AA/Sarah Montgomery; **36tl** AA/Neil Setchfield; **36tr/37tl** AA/Max Jourdan; **36cr/37cl** Courtesy Natural History Museum; **37tr** Courtesy Natural History Museum/Derek Adams; **38t/39tl** Pawel Libera Images/Alamy; **39tr** London Stills; **39cr** AA/Max Jourdan; **40t** David Noton/TTL; **41tr** SJ Images/Alamy; **42l** London Stills; **42tr/43tl** Courtesy St Paul's Cathedral/Peter Smith; **42br/43bl** AA/AA; **43r** AA/Sarah Montgomery; **44l/45r** Courtesy Science Museum; **44tr-44br/45tl-45bl** AA/James Tims; **46l** AA/Richard Turpin; **46/47** AA/Sarah Montgomery; **48tr** Neil Setchfield/Alamy; **48tr/49tl** VIEW Pictures Ltd/Alamy; **49tr** Courtesy Trustees of Sir John Soane's Museum/Derry Moore; **49br** Nigel Dickinson/Alamy; **50tl-50cr/51cl** AA/James Tims; **50tr/51tl** The Courtauld Gallery/James Tims; **51tr** The Courtauld Gallery/James Tims; **52/53tr** AA/Sarah Montgomery; **54tl** AA/Neil Setchfield; **54tr/55tl** AA/James Tims; **54cr/55cl** AA/Sarah Montgomery; **55tr** Courtesy Herzog & de Meuron/Hayes Davidson; **56t/57tl** AA/Clive Sawyer; **56cl** AA/Tim Woodcock; **56cr/57cl** AA/James Tims; **57tr** Courtesy London Duck Tours Ltd; **57cr** AA/James Tims; **58t** AA/Sarah Montgomery; **59** AA/Sarah Montgomery **60t/61tl** Maurice Crooks/Alamy; **61tr** Courtesy Victoria and Albert Museum/Alan Williams; **61cr** Courtesy Victoria and Albert Museum/Richard Waite; **62tl** Tom Mackie/TTL; **62/63** AA/James Tims; **64t** AA/Robert Mort; **66bl** AA/James Tims; **66br** AA/Sarah Montgomery; **67** AA/James Tims; **68b** AA/Neil Setchfield; **69bl** AA/James Tims; **69br** AA/James Tims; **70b** AA/Simon McBride; **71b** AA/Neil Setchfield; **72** AA/James Tims; **73bl** AA/Sarah Montgomery; **73br** Courtesy Zoological Society of London; **74bl** AA/Sarah Montgomery; **74br/75b** AA/James Tims; **76bl** AA/Paul Kenward; **76br** Courtesy Museum of London; **78** AA/Derek Forss; **79bl** AA/Wyn Voysey; **79br** AA/James Tims; **80** AA/Sarah Montgomery; **82tr** AA/James Tims; **82cl** AA/Sarah Montgomery; **82br** AA/Max Jourdan; **83tr** AA/Sarah Montgomery; **83cl** AA/Richard Turpin; **83br** Courtesy EDF Energy London Eye; **86tr** AA/James Tims; **86cr** AA/Sarah Montgomery; **87b** AA/James Tims; **88tr** AA/Neil Setchfield; **88cl** Courtesy Museum of London; **89tr** AA/Sarah Montgomery; **89 lower c** AA/Wyn Voysey; **92tr** Courtesy Museum of London; **92cr** Courtesy St Paul's Cathedral/Peter Smith; **92br** AA/Sarah Montgomery; **93b** Courtesy Transport for London/Hayes Davidson; **94l** Neil Setchfield/Alamy; **94b** The Courtauld Gallery/James Tims; **95** AA/James Tims; **98tr** AA/Neil Setchfield; **98cr** AA/Michael Taylor; **98br** The Courtauld Gallery/James Tims; **100t** Courtesy The National Portrait Gallery/Andrew Putler; **100cr** AA/James Tims; **101t** London Stills; **101bl** AA/Clive Sawyer; **104r top to bottom** i) AA/James Tims; ii) AA/Sarah Montgomery; iii) AA/James Tims; iv) London Stills; v) AA/Sarah Montgomery; vi) AA/Sarah Montgomery; vii) AA/Sarah Montgomery; viii) AA/Neil Setchfield; **105tr** AA/Barrie Smith; **106l** Courtesy Victoria and Albert Museum; **107tr** AA/James Tims; **107b** AA/Sarah Montgomery; **110r top to bottom** i) AA/Paul Kenward; ii) AA/Paul Kenward; iii) AA/Tim Woodcock; iv) AA/James Tims; v) Courtesy Victoria and Albert Museum/Morley von Sternberg; **112t** AA/S and O Mathews; **112br** David Noton/TTL; **113t** AA/S and O Mathews; **113cl** AA/Wyn Voysey; **116tr** AA/AA; **116cr** AA/Max Jourdan; **116br** Courtesy Royal Botanic Gardens, Kew/A.McRobb; **118** AA/James Tims; **120/121 clockwise from top** i) AA/Sarah Montgomery; ii) AA/James Tims; iii) AA/Richard Turpin; iv) AA/Rick Strange; v) AA/Martin Trelawny; vi) AA/Sarah Montgomery; **125br** AA/James Tims; **127br** AA/Sarah Montgomery; **128** AA/James Tims; **130/131 clockwise from top** i) AA/James Tims; ii) AA/James Tims; iii) AA/Max Jourdan; iv) AA/Sarah Montgomery; v) AA/James Tims; vi) AA/James Tims; **134tl** AA/James Tims; **139tr** AA/Richard Turpin; **140** AA/James Tims; **142r top to bottom** i) AA/AA; ii) AA/Max Jourdan; iii) AA/Neil Setchfield; iv) AA/James Tims; **146bl** AA/Neil Setchfield; **146br** AA/James Tims; **148tl** AA/Neil Setchfield; **152** AA/Robert Mort; **154r top to bottom** i) AA/Wyn Voysey; ii) AA/James Tims; iii) OneOff Travel/Alamy; iv) VIEW Pictures Ltd/Alamy; 157b AA/Sarah Montgomery; **158tl** AA/James Tims; **160** AA/Sarah Montgomery.

Every effort has been made to trace the copyright holders, and we apologise in advance for any unintentional omissions or errors. We would be pleased to apply any corrections in a following edition of this publication.

174

Published by AA Publishing, a trading name of AA Media Limited, whose registered office is Fanum House, Basing View, Basingstoke, Hampshire RG21 4EA. Registered number 06112600.

© **AA Media Limited 2015**
First published 1996
New edition 2015

WRITTEN BY Louise Nicholson
ADDITIONAL WRITING AND UPDATED BY Sue Dobson
SERIES EDITOR Clare Ashton
COVER DESIGN Tracey Freestone, Nick Johnston
DESIGN WORK Tracey Freestone
IMAGE RETOUCHING AND REPRO Ian Little

Colour separation by AA Digital Department
Printed and bound by Leo Paper Products, China

A CIP catalogue record for this book is available from the British Library.

ISBN 978-0-7495-7624-0

We have tried to ensure accuracy in this guide, but things do change, so please let us know if you have any comments at travelguides@theAA.com.

A05237
Mapping © Crown copyright and database rights 2015 Ordnance Survey. 100021153

Titles in the Series

- Amsterdam
- Barcelona
- Boston
- Budapest
- Dublin
- Florence
- Istanbul
- Las Vegas
- London
- Madrid
- New York
- Orlando
- Paris
- Rome
- San Francisco
- Singapore
- Venice